Co-creation

Anastasia herself has stated that this book consists of words and phrases in combinations *which have a beneficial effect on the reader.* This has been attested by the letters received to date from tens of thousands of readers all over the world.

If you wish to gain as full an appreciation as possible of the ideas, thoughts and images set forth here, as well as experience the benefits that come with this appreciation, we recommend you find a quiet place for your reading where there is the least possible interference from artificial noises (motor traffic, radio, TV, household appliances etc.). *Natural sounds,* on the other hand — the singing of birds, for example, or the patter of rain, or the rustle of leaves on nearby trees — may be a welcome accompaniment to the reading process.

,50

THE RINGING CEDARS SERIES • BOOK FOUR

Co-creation

Vladimir Megré

Translated from the Russian by **John Woodsworth**
Edited by **Dr Leonid Sharashkin**

RINGING
CEDARS
PRESS

KAHULUI • HAWAII • USA

FSC Recycled
Supporting responsible use
of forest resources
www.fsc.org Cert no. SW-COC-002283
© 1996 Forest Stewardship Council

100%

Publisher's Cataloging-In-Publication Data

Megre, V. (Vladimir), 1950-
  [Sotvorenie. English.]
  Co-creation / Vladimir Megré ; translated from the Russian by John
Woodsworth ; edited by Leonid Sharashkin. — 2nd ed., rev.

  p. : ill. ; cm. — (The ringing cedars series ; bk. 4)

  ISBN: 978-0-9801812-3-4

  1. Spirituality. 2. Nature—Religious aspects. 3. Human ecology. I.
Woodsworth, John, 1944- II. Sharashkin, Leonid. III. Title. IV. Title:
Sotvorenie. English. V. Series: Megre, V. (Vladimir), 1950- Ringing cedars
series, bk. 4.

GF80 .M44 2008d
304.2   2008923349

Contents

CHAPTER ONE

All this exists right now!

"I shall tell you about *co-creation*, Vladimir, and then everyone will be able to provide an answer to his own questions. Please listen carefully, Vladimir, and write about the Creator's great co-creation. Listen and try to understand with all your Soul the aspirations of the Divine dream."

After uttering these words, Anastasia fell into a silent distraction. She looked at me but said not a word. Her distraction was probably due to her feeling or noticing in my facial expression signs of incredulity in what she might have to say about Co-creation, about God.

But really, how could I — or anyone else, for that matter — not entertain at least some measure of incredulity? What could not this passionate recluse dream up next?! She doesn't have any historical proofs to offer. If anyone can talk convincingly about the past, then surely that would be the historians and archæologists. And there's lots of talk about God in the Bible and in the books of other denominations. In all kinds of books. Only for some reason, when they talk of God, they can't seem to agree. Might not that be on account of the fact that nobody has any convincing proofs?

"There *are* proofs, Vladimir," Anastasia suddenly broke in confidently and excitedly in answer to my silent question.

"And where are they?"

"All the proofs, all the truths in the Universe are preserved for ever in every human soul. Lies and falsehoods cannot survive for any length of time. They are exposed by the soul. That is why so many different kinds of religious treatises are thrown at Man.[1] Lies constantly need new disguises to survive. And that is why mankind is constantly changing its social structures, trying to find in them the truth it has lost, yet only distancing itself from the truth even more."

"But who has proved, and how, that each one contains the truth within? In Man's soul or any other part? And if it is indeed there, then why does it stay hidden?"

"On the contrary, not a single day goes by but in the sight of each one of us the truth strives to bring itself out. Life around us is eternal and it is through the truth that eternal life comes about."

Anastasia quickly pressed the palms of her hands to the ground, ran them over the grass and then held them out to me.

"Look, Vladimir, perhaps these will dispel your doubts once and for all."

I looked, and saw in her outstretched hands seeds of grass, a small cedar nut, and some sort of bug crawling. I asked her:

"And what does all this mean? The nut, for example?"

"Look, Vladimir, such a tiny wee kernel, and yet if you plant it in the ground, it grows into a majestic cedar. Not an oak, not a maple, not a rose, but only a cedar. The cedar in turn gives birth to a kernel just like this, and it will contain, just as the very first one did, all the information about its pristine origins. And if millions of years ago or millions of years from now a kernel like this makes contact with the earth, still, only a cedar will sprout out of the ground. In it, in every kernel of God's perfect creation, all possible information has been fully implanted by the Creator. Millions of years may go by, but

---

[1]*Man* — Throughout the Ringing Cedars Series, the word *Man* with a capital *M* is used to refer to a human being of either gender. For details on the word's usage and the important distinction between *Man* and *human being* please see the Translator's Preface to Book 1.

the Creator's information will never be erased. And Man, the apex of creation, has been given everything by the Creator at the moment of co-creation. All truths and all future achievements have been inculcated by the Father, inspired by a grand dream, in His beloved child."

"Well then, how do we attain that truth, in the final analysis? From somewhere within ourselves? From our kidneys, our heart or our brain?"

"From our feelings. You should try to determine the truth with your feelings. Trust yourself to them. Free yourself from mercenary dogmas."

"Well, okay, if you know something, say it. Perhaps somebody will be able to understand you with their *own* feelings. What is God, for example? Can scholars draw a portrait of Him with some kind of scientific formula?"

"A scientific formula? A formula would extend many times around the Earth, and when it stopped, another would be given birth. God is no less in worth than what can be born in one's thought. He is the firmament and the empty space, and that which cannot be seen. There is no sense in trying to understand Him with the mind, however keen. Take all the formulas on the Earth and all the information in the Universe as a whole and squeeze them into the tiny kernel of your soul and turn them into feelings, and let your feelings then unfold."

"But what am I supposed to feel? Talk in terms more simple, clearer and more real."

"Oh, help me, God!" Anastasia pleaded. "Help me with the creation of a worthy image out of today's word combinations."

"Well now, not enough words, eh? Why don't you go take a look at a dictionary? It's got all the words people use today."

"All the words available *at the moment*. But modern books do not contain the words your forefathers used to describe God."

"Are you talking about Old Church Slavonic[2] words?"

"And even earlier. Before the Old Church Slavonic alphabet was invented, there was a means by which people set down their thoughts for their descendants."

"What are you talking about, Anastasia? Everyone knows that our proper writing system came from two Orthodox monks. Their names were... something, I can't remember."

"Cyril and Methodius, perhaps, you have in mind?"

"Yes. They created our kind of writing system, after all."

"It would be more accurate to say: they *changed* the writing system of our forefathers and foremothers."

"What d'you mean, they 'changed' it?"

"They were following orders. To make sure the culture of the Slavs would be forgotten for ever. To make sure the remnants of knowledge of our pristine origins would disappear from human memory, and a new culture would be born, so that our peoples would subject themselves to different priests."

"What have writing systems and a new culture got to do with that?"

"Suppose children today were taught to speak and write a foreign tongue, and forbidden to express themselves in the one they already know. Tell me, Vladimir, how would your grandchildren learn about events of our present day? In people deprived of a knowledge of the past it is easy to inculcate new teachings, simply by treating them as important. And

[2]*Old Church Slavonic* — a literary language developed from the Slavic dialect used by two monks named Saints Cyril [*Kirill*] and Methodius [*Mefodii*], who first translated the Bible into a Slavic tongue in the 10th century A.D. and invented an alphabet (which many people identify as *Cyrillic*) wherein to write down their translation. It was used as the liturgical language of the Russian Orthodox Church up until the 12th century. Its present-day derivative is known simply as *Church Slavonic,* and is still used in Orthodox liturgy today.

they can tell them anything they like about their forebears. Once the language had gone, culture went along with it. That was the aim, at least. But those who formulated that aim were wholly unaware that the sprouts of truth remained unseen for ever in the human soul. All it takes is to drink in a single drop of dew so pure for the sprout to grow and mature. Look, Vladimir. Please, accept my words, and try to feel what lies behind them."

As Anastasia spoke, she would either slow down her speech or quickly rattle off whole phrases at a time, or else suddenly fall silent for a moment, ponder something for a moment, and then pluck unfamiliar, drawn-out phrases literally out of the air. And occasionally a word or two I had never heard before would weave their way into what she was saying. But each time she said an unclear or unknown word, she seemed to give a start and replace it with a correct or more understandable variant. And it always appeared as though she were trying to prove something whenever she talked of God:

"Everybody knows Man is the image and likeness of God. But in what respect? Where are God's characteristic traits within you? Have you ever thought of that?"

"No, not really," I admitted. "Never had any occasion to. Why don't you describe them yourself?"

"When a Man, exhausted after his daily cares, lies down to sleep, when he ceases to feel his weary body, his set of invisible energies and his 'second self'[3] leave the body to some degree. And at that moment earthly limitations do not exist for them. They know no time or space. In less than a second, your consciousness crosses all the distances in the Universe. And your complex of feelings senses past and future events, analyses them, measures them against the present day and dreams on. All this means that Man feels the unfathomable

---

[3]*second self* — see Book 3, Chapter 15: "A bird for discovering one's soul".

Divine universal creation not only with his flesh. His God-given thought is at work creating afresh. Human thought alone is capable of creating other worlds or changing what has been created.

"Sometimes a person will cry out in their sleep when they are scared by something. Their complex of feelings, free from earthly cares, is frightened by events of the past or the future.

"Sometimes a person creates in their sleep. Their creations strive, quickly or slowly, to embody themselves in earthly form. And how ugly a form they take or how harmoniously they shine forth depends wholly or partly on the degree to which inspiration plays a role in their creations. On the degree to which all aspects are taken into account in all their accuracy and detail at the moment of creation. On the degree to which inspiration empowers your Divine 'self'.

"In the whole Universe creation is something inherent in God alone, and in God's son, Man.

"God's thought serves as the principle of all. His dream is transformed into living matter so that it may be seen. And human actions are preceded by the human dream.

"The opportunities for creation are equal for all the people of the Earth. It is only that people use their opportunities in different ways. Here Man is accorded full freedom. And freedom he has!

"Tell me now, Vladimir, what kind of dreams do God's children have today? You yourself, your friends and acquaintances, for example? For what purpose do they use their creative dreams? What purpose do *you* use them for?"

"Me? Hmm... how d'you mean, for what purpose? Just like everyone else, I've tried to make more money so I can somehow get my life on a solid footing. I got myself a car — several, in fact. Plus a lot of other things I need to get by — good furniture, for example."

"And that is it? Is that all you have used your creative, God-given dream for?"

"That's what just about everyone uses it for."

"For what?"

"For money! How can you live without money? To have a decent set of clothes to wear, to eat a little better, buy things, get something to drink. What could be clearer than that? And you ask what for!"

"Something to eat, something to drink — you realise, Vladimir, that all this has been given to everyone in abundance, right from the very beginning."

"Given? Well, then, where did it disappear to after that?"

"Think for yourself: where might it have gone?"

"Well, I would imagine the original clothing simply got ragged and worn out, and the original food got eaten up æons ago. Times are different now, clothing fashions have changed, along with tastes for food."

"Vladimir, God gave His son indestructible garments, and his food reserves are not the kind that can ever be exhausted."

"So where's all this today?"

"It has all been preserved, it exists right now."

"Then tell me where. Where do I find the hiding-places where so many supplies are stored up even today?"

"You shall see. They shall be seen. Only look with your feelings. Only with your feelings will you be able to grasp the essence of the creation of God's dream."

CHAPTER TWO

The beginning of creation

"Picture what it was like in the very beginning. There was as yet no Earth. There was as yet no matter to reflect the light of the Universe. But still, even as now, the Universe was filled with a great multitude of diverse energies. Living energy elements thought in the dark, and created in the dark. They needed no external light-source. Within themselves, for themselves, they shone. And each contained everything — thought, feelings and the energy of aspiration. Yet still there were differences among them. In each one a single form of energy predominated. Just as now, the Universe included an element of destruction and an element which creates life. And other elements involved a multitude of various shadings, similar to human feelings. There was no way these elements of the Universe could come into contact with each other. Within each element multiple energies created movement — either languidly creeping or, all at once, lightning-swift on the dot. What was self-created within each one could also destroy itself on the spot. Their pulsations did not alter the Cosmos — visible they were not — and each considered that they were alone in space. Alone!

"Uncertain of their purpose, they were unable to bring about any lasting creation that might give satisfaction. And so in a time of stagnation without limitation there were these pulsations, but there was no overall motion or action of any kind.

"And all at once, as by an impulse, each element was touched by *communication*! All of them at once, throughout the unfathomable Universe. Throughout those complexes of living energy one suddenly began illuminating the rest. Whether the complex was old or young could not be expressed in ordinary tongues. Whether it arose from the vacuum of space or from the spark of all the possibilities one could imagine is not important. Whatever its semblance, the resulting complex bore a most striking resemblance to Man! To Man who is still living today! It was similar to his second self. Not the material, but the eternal, sacred self. The living energy of its aspirations and dreams first began to lightly touch all elements in the Universe. And he alone was so fervent in his devotion that he was able to bring all sensations and feelings into locomotion. The sounds of communication began to resound through the Universe. And if the first sounds were to be expressed through translation into modern words, we would feel the sense of questions and answers. From all across the unfathomable Universe one question was uttered by all, addressed only to Him:

"'What do you so fervently desire?' everyone enquired.

"And He, confident in His dream, replied:

"'Conjoint creation and joy for all from its contemplation.'

"'And what may bring joy to everyone in the Universe?'

"'Birth!'

"'The birth of what? Each one of us has been self-sufficient for as long as we can recall.'

"'A birth in which will be included particles of all!'

"'How is it possible to reunite in a single whole that which is all-destructive and all-constructive at the same time?'

"'Through opposing forms of energy, after first bringing them into line, balancing them in one's self, you see!'

"'And, to achieve this, who so strong would there be?'

"'Me.'

"'But there is the energy of doubt. Doubt will attempt to decoy and destroy you, and the diverse multitude of energies will tear you into tiny particles. No one can unite and hold opposites in a single whole.'

"'But there is also the energy of confidence. When confidence and doubt are equal, they will facilitate exactitude and beatitude for future co-creation.'

"'And how do you call yourself?'

"'I am God. I shall be able to deploy particles of all your diverse energies within Myself. I shall stay great! I shall create! To the whole Universe creation shall bring forth joy!'

"From all quarters of the Universe all elements simultaneously released the multitude of their energies into Him alone. And each endeavoured to gain ascendancy over the rest, so that it alone might establish itself as supreme in its new home.

"Thus began the great struggle of all the forms of energy in the Universe. There is no measure of time or space to describe the scale of that struggle. Calm returned only when in each one's consciousness one fact gleamed: that nothing could be higher or stronger than the One energy of the Universe — the energy of the Divine dream.

"God possessed the energy of the dream. He was able to take in and compile all within Himself, bring all into balance, reconcile opposites and begin to create. And to create still within Himself. Indeed, in His creating of future creations still within Himself, He cherished each detail with speed on a measureless scale, and worked out the interrelationships with everything else for each and every creation. He did it all alone. Alone in the darkness of the unfathomable Universe. Alone he set into motion the diverse energies of the whole Universe. The uncertainty of the outcome frightened everyone and removed them a distance from the Creator. The Creator found Himself standing in empty space. And that empty space was expanding.

"A deathly cold appeared. Dank fear and alienation held sway around, while He alone beheld the awesome dawn of each new day, heard the singing of birds, and breathed the sweet fragrance of the blossoming of the ground. With His fervent dream He alone unfolded His marvellous creations in their sheen.

"'Stop!' they pleaded. 'You are in empty space. You are going to explode! How do You contain the energy within Yourself? Nobody is helping You squeeze or contract, and now Your only course is to explode. But if You have a moment remaining, stop! You must act to gently release your creative energies.'

"And He replied:

"'My dreams! I will not betray My pact with them! For them I will continue to contract and accelerate My energies, My powers. My dreams! In them I see the ants hurrying and scurrying across the grass, among the flowers. And the eagle in his bold ascent into the sky is teaching his young how to fly.'

"With His own unfathomable energy God accelerated in Himself the motion of all the diverse energies of the Universe as a whole. Inspiration squeezed them into a small kernel in His Soul.

"And all at once He sensed a touch. Everywhere, from all quarters in turn, He felt the burn of a new unfamiliar energy, and then it withdrew to warm Him with its warmth from a distance, filling all with some kind of new power. And all that was previously empty space suddenly began to radiate with grace. And the Universe resounded with new sounds, when God enquired with tender ecstasy:

"'Who are you? What kind of energy are you?'

"And He heard the words of Music in reply:

"'The Energy of Love and Inspiration am I.'

"'A particle of you is within Me. It alone is able to restrain and cage the energy of disdain, hatred and rage.'

"'You are God. Your energy — the dream of Your Soul — has been able to bring everything into the harmony of the whole. And if my particle has been of assistance there, then hear me out, O God, and to help me be prepared.'

"'What do you desire? Why have you touched Me with all the power of your fire?'

"'I have realised that I am Love. I cannot remain simply a particle of... I desire to give my whole self to Your Soul. I know, so as not to disrupt the harmony of good and evil, You will not admit me as a whole. But I shall fill with myself the empty space around You. I shall warm with my cheer all the room within and around You. You shall not be touched by the cold of the Universe and its gloom — it shall not even come near.'

"'What is going on here? What indeed? You have begun to shine even brighter!'

"'I am not doing this alone. This is the presence of Your energy! Your Soul! It is only being reflected by me. Your reflected light comes back, back to your invisible Inner Self.'

"Aflame with courage and aspiration, God, inspired by Love, exclaimed:

"'Everything is proceeding with acceleration. Everything is astir in Me. O, how marvellous is inspiration here above! And now let the dreams of My creation come to fruition in most radiant Love!'"

CHAPTER THREE

The first appearance of *you*

"The Earth! The core of the whole Universe and the centre of everything appeared as the planet Earth loomed in sight! And all at once, along with it loomed the stars, the Sun and the Moon. The invisible creative light radiating from the Earth found its reflection in them.

"In the Universe a new plan of existence appeared for the first time! A material plan, and how it did shine!

"Up to the moment the Earth appeared, nobody and nothing possessed visible matter. While the Earth came into contact with everything in the Universe, it was an independent body, too.

"It was a self-sufficient creation. Things that lived all around, things that grew in the ground, things that swam in the sea and things that flew on high did not die or disappear somewhere. Even decomposition brought forth flies, and flies became food for other life, and everything fused together into a single magnificent life.

"In their excitement and astonishment all the entities of the Universe began looking to the Earth. The Earth came into contact with everything, but nobody was able to touch it.

"With God a sense of inner inspiration surged apace. And in the light of Love, which had filled the empty space, the Divine being changed its design, and took the form which in time became known as the human body.

"The Divine thought worked with no sense of speed or time. Indeed, it worked infinitely faster than all the diverse energies of thought and created with inspiration!

And again another creation which was still invisible, still within itself.

"All at once the illumination flared up, and the energy of Love gave a quiver of agitation, as if set aflame with its newly felt heat. And in joyous elation God exclaimed:

"'Look, O Universe, look! Behold my son! Man! He stands upon the Earth. He is material! And in him are particles of all the diverse energies of the Universe. He dwells on all the planes of being. My image and likeness he is, and in him are particles of all your diverse energies... So love him! I urge you: love him!

"'My son shall bring joy to all living on the Earth. He is creation! He is birth! He is all of all! He will create a new creation, and will transform into infinity his ever-repeating regeneration.

"'When alone, or when infinitely multiplied, he emits invisible light, merging it into a whole, he will rule the Universe. He will endow everything with the joy of life. I have given him everything that is Mine, and will furthermore give him for his own all that may be thought at a future time.'

"Thus for the first time you stood alone on the splendid Earth," Anastasia ended her narrative.

"Who are you talking about?" I queried. "About me?"

"About you, Vladimir, and about anyone who happens to see these lines you shall be writing down."

"How so, Anastasia? There's a complete disconnect here. How can all my readers stand on a spot where you say only one person was standing. And it talks about that in the Bible. There was just one Man at first — Adam, he was called. And you yourself said God created just one Man."

"Quite correct, Vladimir. But look and see: it is from that one that we all have come. His particle, and the information contained therein, has been infused into all others who have been given birth upon the Earth. And if your willing thought is ready to cast aside all your worldly cares, then all the feelings held up to now in that tiny particle will be felt. It has been there all along, and remembers everything. It is in you right now and in every Man living upon the Earth. Let it unfold, let yourself feel what you have seen, and you who are in turn reading these lines at the moment, you shall feel what you saw at the very beginning of your journey through time."

"Oh wow! Then is it true that everyone living today was there, on that Earth, right at the very beginning?"

"Yes. But on *this* Earth, not on 'that' one. It is only that the Earth looked different back then."

"And is there a single term by which we can be called?"

"You are probably more accustomed to hearing the name *Adam*? I shall use it, but picture it as referring to you. And let everyone picture themselves when they come across that name. I shall use some words to help in this."

"Yes, please do. For some reason I still have only a rather faint idea of how I might have appeared in those times."

"To make it easier, picture yourself as entering a garden on the border between summer and spring — a garden in which there are also the fruits of autumn. There are also beings here which you are seeing for the first time. It is hard to take everything in at one glance, when it is all so new and everything radiates perfection. But recall how you, Adam, saw your first flower and concentrated your thought upon it. On a very tiny flower.

"It was cornflower blue, the petals were smooth and made up of lines. The petals gently glowed, as though reflecting in themselves the light of the sky. And you, Adam, sat down beside the flower, admiring this creation. But no matter how long you looked at it, the flower's appearance was constantly changing. A breeze caressed the flower, making it sway on its slender stem, and the petals quivered under the Sun's rays, changing the angle of reflection, giving new shadings to its tender hues. When the petals were not trembling in the breeze, they seemed to be waving to the Man in greeting, or moving in time to the music ringing in the soul. And the flower gave off a most delicate fragrance in its efforts to embrace you, the Man.

"All at once Adam heard a mighty roar and, rising, turned in the direction of the sound. In the distance an enormous lion was standing with his lioness. And the lion announced himself with his roar to everything around.

"Adam's gaze became entranced by the lion's stately and powerful stance, crowned by a bushy mane. No sooner had the lion spied Adam than the creature bounded toward him with mighty steps, the lioness right behind him. Adam could not help but be impressed by the play of their powerful muscles. Three metres from the Man the creatures came to rest. Man's gaze caressed them, a feeling of delight was emanating from the Man, while the lion, sensing the gentle calm, settled to the ground in delight. The lioness lay down beside him, keeping perfectly still so as not to interfere with the warm and gracious light emanating from the Man.

"Adam ran his fingers through the lion's mane, examined and touched the claws of his mighty paws, put his hand on his great white fangs and smiled when the lion purred with delight."

"Anastasia," I couldn't help asking, "what kind of light first emanated from the Man to stop the lion from tearing him apart? And why is there no such radiance today? Nobody emits light that way today."

"Vladimir, have you not noticed what a huge difference there is even today? Man's gaze distinguishes all that is earthly — the little blades of grass and flowers, the wild beasts and the rocks with sluggish thinking. It is curious, mysterious, full of unexplained power. Man's gaze can be calming. And yet it can also wrap all living creatures in the cold of destruction.

Tell me, has it ever happened that you have been warmed by someone's gaze? Or perhaps someone's eyes have caused you inner discomfort?"

"Yes, it's happened. You can actually feel someone watching you. You can feel a pleasant gaze, or one that is not so pleasant."

"There, you see... that means you too know that a calming gaze will create a sense of warmth within you. And that an opposite gaze will bring a feeling of cold and destruction. But Man's gaze was many times stronger during those first days upon Earth. The Creator saw to it that all life aspired to be warmed by this gaze."

"And where has all the strength of Man's gaze gone now?"

"It has not all gone. Enough of it is still around, but vanity, superficial thinking, a different speed of thought, a misapprehension of basic concepts and apathy have darkened perception, and prevented it from opening up to what everybody expects of Man. Inside each one of us a warm heart abides. Oh, if only each one of us could open it wide to everything! All reality could then be transmogrified into a magnificent pristine garden."

"Is this possible with everyone? Just as in the beginning with Adam? Could something like that actually transpire?"

"Everything may be born, which is to what human thought, merging from all into one, aspires.

"When Adam was alone, the power of his mind was equal to what today is found in all mankind."

"Aha! That's why the lion was afraid of him!"

"The lion was not afraid of the Man, not a trace. The lion was bowing before the light of grace. All life aspires to know this grace, which Man alone is capable of creating. For this all life, and not only upon the Earth, is ready to perceive Man as a friend, a brother, a god. Parents always strive to instil in their children all the very best abilities. Only parents sincerely want their children's abilities to exceed their own. The

Creator has wholly given Man — His son and creation — all
to which He Himself aspired in a burst of inspiration. And
if all are able to understand that God is perfect, then may all
feel exactly who God the Creator planned to create His child
to be — His beloved son, or Man. And how He feared no bur-
den of responsibility, and how he undertook never to abandon
His creation, having uttered the words that have come down
to us over the millions of years: 'He is My son, this Man. He
is My image! My likeness!'"

"Does that mean that God wanted His son, His creation —
Man, in other words, to be stronger than Himself?"

"All parents' aspirations may be seen as a confirmation of this."

"Well then, did Adam justify God's hopes for him on his
first day? What transpired after the meeting with the lion?
What did he set about to do?"

"Adam aspired to know all living things. To define the
name and the purpose or need for each living creature. Some
of these were solved quickly, others he became involved with
for quite a time indeed. For example, before the Sun set on
the first day he was attempting to define the purpose of the
brontosaurus, but here he did not succeed. And so the brontosaurus disappeared from the face of the Earth for all time."

"Disappeared — why?"

"It disappeared because Man did not define its purpose."

"That brontosaurus — is that the one that's several times
bigger than an elephant?"

"Yes, bigger than an elephant it was, and little wings it had,
and a little head on a long neck that could spew flame out of
its jaws."

"Just like in a fairy tale. The folk tale about the Gorynytch
Serpent,' for example, which spewed fire, too. But that's a
fairy tale, not something real."

"Sometimes folk tales tell about a past reality metaphorically, but sometimes they can be quite accurate."

"Really? And just what would such a monster be made of? How could fire come out of the jaws of a real living creature? Or is the fire to be taken metaphorically? Let's say, for instance, to portray a monster breathing hatred?"

"The huge brontosaurus was good, not evil. Its huge size served to compensate for its enormous weight."

"How can its huge size serve to lighten its weight?"

"The more a hot-air balloon is filled with whatever is lighter than air, the lighter it is."

"Well, what has that got to do with the brontosaurus? *It's* not a hot-air balloon!"

"The brontosaurus was indeed an enormous living hot-air balloon. Its skeleton was constructed of very light-weight material, while its insides contained little in the way of organs. Just as with a balloon, its insides were empty, except they were constantly being filled with a gas that was lighter than air. With a leap and a flap of its wings, the brontosaurus actually managed to fly a bit. When there was an excessive build-up of gas, it breathed it out through its mouth. Flint-like fangs protruded from its jaws, and their friction could create a spark and ignite the gas welling up from its abdominal cavity, sending fire out of its mouth."

"Hmm! But hold on there, hold on — just who kept filling it with gas?"

"Listen to me, Vladimir: the gas was produced all by itself inside as its food was being digested."

"Impossible! Gas exists only in the bowels of the Earth. That's where it is extracted from, then they use it to fill

---

[1]*Gorynytch Serpent* — a fire-breathing dragon in Russian folk tales, with as many as twelve heads, associated with fire and water, capable of flight, yet making its lair in caves and holes in the ground wherein to hide its captured treasure, including kidnapped princesses. *Gorynytch* literally means "son of a Mountain", referring to its great size.

propane tanks or send it through pipes to people's kitchen stoves. But from food — is it really that simple?"

"Yes, Vladimir, it is really that simple."

"I can't believe in something that simple, neither will anyone else. And that means everything you've told me, for that matter, not just about the brontosaurus, but everything else too — nobody's going to believe it! So I shan't write about this."

"What is it, Vladimir? Do you think I am capable of being mistaken? Of lying?"

"Well, I don't know about the lying part, but you're definitely mistaken about the gas."

"I am not mistaken."

"Then prove it."

"Vladimir — do you not realise that your stomach, and other people's stomachs, produce the same kind of gas even today?"

"Impossible."

"You can prove it for yourself. Just take a match and light the gas when it comes out of you."

"What d'you mean, 'out of me'? Out of where? Where would I light the match?"

Anastasia broke out laughing and, still laughing, said:

"What are you, a little child? Think for yourself — it is a private experience."

I thought about this gas from time to time. And for some reason the thought began to eat away at me. And finally I decided to try the experiment. I tried it directly I returned from my visit with Anastasia. It worked! And now I think back even more vividly on what she said about Adam's first days — or, rather, *our* first days on the Earth. And I get the feeling that somehow we have forgotten to take with us today something from those days. Or maybe it was just me that forgot. That's something each one can decide for himself when he learns how Man spent his first day on the Earth. This is how Anastasia described it.

Chapter Four

The first day

"Adam was interested in everything. Each blade of grass, each intricate little bug, the birds in the sky above, and water. The first sight of a stream, its transparent running water sparkling in the Sun, filled him with wonder and admiration, and in it he could behold life in its infinite manifestations. When Adam bent down to touch the water, his hand was immediately embraced by the current which caressed all the folds of his skin and drew him in. Upon immersing himself in the water he found his body becoming lighter. The gurgling water supported him and comforted his whole body. Splashing the water in the air with his hands, he was delighted to see the play of the Sun's bright rays in each and every drop, before the drops were once more received back into the stream. And it was with a great sense of delight that Adam drank the water from the stream. And before the Sun set he gladly contemplated, and bathed again, and meditated."

"Hold on, there, Anastasia. You mentioned him drinking, but did Adam eat anything the whole day? What food did he eat?"

"All around him were a multitude of fruits with a variety of tastes, berries and edible grasses. But during those first days Adam felt no sense of hunger. He remained satisfied with fresh air alone."

"With fresh air? But you can't live on air. There's even a saying about that."

"One certainly cannot live on the air Man breathes today. Today's air is dying, and is often harmful for one's body and soul. You mentioned the saying that one cannot live on air, but there is another saying: 'I have been fed by air alone', which corresponds to what was available to Man in the beginning. Adam was born in a marvellous garden, and the air surrounding him did not contain a single harmful particle. Pollen had been dissolved into that air, along with drops of purest dew."

"Pollen? What kind of pollen?"

"Pollen from flowers and grasses, from trees and fruit, which diffused fragrances into the air. Some came from those close by, while breezes brought others from distant places. Back then Man was not distracted from his great works by any problems of finding food. He was fed by everything around him through the air. This was the way it was all designed by the Creator right from the very beginning, so that all life on Earth should strive to please Man, and the air and the water and the breeze would be life-giving, under the impulse of love."

"You're right about one thing: air can be very harmful, but Man invented the air conditioner. It purifies the air of dangerous particles. And people sell mineral water in bottles. So, you see, the problems of air and water have been solved — at least for the many people who aren't poor."

"Alas, Vladimir, the air conditioner does not solve any problems. It keeps back harmful particles, yes, but the air continues to die. The water preserved in air-tight bottles dies for lack of fresh air. All it does is feed the old cells of the body. For new birth, so that the cells of your body may constantly renew themselves, *living* air and water are needed."

CHAPTER FIVE

Problems confirming the perfection of life

"Adam had all that?" I asked in amazement.

"Yes, he did! This is why his thought moved so quickly. In a relatively short period of time he was able to define everything's purpose. One hundred and eighteen years swept by like a single day."

"A hundred and eighteen years! Adam lived all by himself to such a ripe old age?"

"All by himself lived Adam, the first Man, caught up in all sorts of interesting projects. A hundred and eighteen years did not bring him age, but a blossoming of life."

"Well, a person's pretty old at a hundred and eighteen — he's known as an 'old-timer', at the mercy of all sorts of diseases and ailments."

"That might be so now, Vladimir, but back then Man was not troubled by diseases. Every one of his cells enjoyed a longer span of life, and if a cell became weary, that meant it was destined to die, but right away a new cell, full of energy, appeared in its place. Man's body was able to live as many years as his spirit or soul wished."

"And how come the Man of today can't wish himself to live a little longer?"

"By his moment-by-moment actions he is cutting short his lifespan, and death is something thought up by Man."

"What do you mean, 'thought up'? Death comes all by itself. Against Man's will."

"When you smoke tobacco or drink alcohol, when you drive

into a city which pollutes the air with the stench of burning fumes, when you use lifeless food and let yourself be eaten away by bitterness, tell me, Vladimir, who, if not yourself, is hastening your death?"

"Well, that kind of life is pretty common for everyone today."

"But Man is free to choose. Everyone builds his own life for himself and determines his lifespan moment by moment."

"So, you're saying that back then, in paradise, there weren't any problems?"

"Problems, if they arose at all, were resolved not in a harmful direction, but in such a way as to confirm the perfection of life."

CHAPTER SIX

First encounter

"One day when he was a hundred and eighteen years old, Adam did not become excited with the Spring upon waking with the dawn. And he did not rise, as he usually did, to greet the Sun's brightening rays.

"Above him astride a leafy branch the nightingale trilled his song. But his singing only made Adam turn over on his other side.

"Before his eyes Spring filled space with a quiet tremolo, the gurgling stream called out to Adam in his bed, while swallows made sport overhead. Fanciful clouds heralded each new unfolding scene. From grasses, flowers, bushes and trees the gentlest fragrance rushed to embrace the Man. Oh, how God wondered then what was taking place! Amidst Spring's resplendent glory, under the deep-blue skies of his earthly creation, his son, the Man, had become sorrowful and despondent. His beloved child dwelt not in gladness but in sadness. Could any scene be more agonising for a loving father?

"One hundred and eighteen years on, long after creation, the dormant throng of Divine energies suddenly swarmed into motion. The whole Universe listened in shocked surprise. Such acceleration as had never been seen before glistened in the aura of the energy of Love, so intensely that all life caught the sense at once: a new creation had been thought of by God. But what could possibly be originated after creation had already reached the limit of inspiration? This was something that surpassed all comprehension. And still God's thought kept growing in acceleration. And the Energy of Love whispered in muted tones:

"'Once more You have set everything in inspired motion. Your universal energies are setting space on fire. How is it that You do not explode or consume yourself in such fervour and desire? Where are You heading? To what are You aspiring? I no longer shine with Your light. Look, O my God, I burn with Your essence, I turn planets into stars. Stop! You have already created all the best. Stop, and Your son's grief will evanesce, it will disappear. Stop, O my God!'

"But God did not hear the plea of Love. And paid no attention to the jeers of the elements of the Universe. Like a young and enthusiastic sculptor, He continued accelerating all the diverse energies in motion. And all at once, a dawn of never before imaginable beauty burst forth, delineating itself through the vast unfathomable Universe, and all creation gasped, and God Himself whispered in exultation:

"'Behold, O Universe, behold! Behold my daughter stands amidst the created creatures of the Earth! How perfect her features are, the finest by a thousandfold! She shall be worthy of My son. A creation more perfect than hers will never come. In her is the image and likeness of Me, each particle of yours in her will always be — so love her with a love so pure and free!

"'She and he! My son and daughter shall bring extended joy to every living thing! And shall build on every plane of being resplendent universal worlds!'

"From the little hill, over dew-washed grass, on the festive day in the Sun's morning ray the maiden to Adam came. With a pace full of grace and a form so slender, the bends of her body smooth and tender, in the hues of her skin there shined the light of the dawn Divine. Closer and closer she neared. And then she appeared! In front of Adam, reclining on the grass, the maiden arose.

"The breeze smoothed out her golden braids, her forehead to expose. The Universe held its breath, completely awed. O, how beauteous is her face — Thy creation, O God!

"Adam, reclining on the grass, glanced up at the maiden who had appeared beside him, gave a yawn, turned away and closed his eyes.

"All the elements in the Universe then heard — no, not words — they heard how listlessly Adam reacted in his thought to the new creation of God:

"'Well, there it is, yet another creation of some kind has come to mind. It is nothing new, you see, just another entity that looks something like me. Horses have joints in their knees more supple and sturdy than these. The leopard has skin so much brighter and livelier to please. And what's more, she arrived without invitation, on the very day I was going to offer the ants a new designation.'

"And Eve, standing a while beside Adam, went over to a pool in the stream, sat down on the bank by the bushes and caught a gleam of her reflection in the still, cool water.

"And the elements of the Universe began to intone their murmurings, and their thoughts merged into one: 'Two perfections have not managed to achieve an appreciation of each other. There is no perfection in God's creation.'

"And only the energy of Love, alone amidst the murmurings of the Universe, tried to protect the Creator with itself. God was enveloped in its radiance. Everybody knew: never had the energy of Love involved itself in rationalisation. Unseen and unheard, it was ever wandering apace through the unfathomed reaches of space. But why was it now, so totally and with no retention, encircling God again with its radiance? Paying no attention to the intonings of the Universe, here it was, warming and comforting through its radiance alone.

"'You can rest, O Great Creator, and impart Your education into the heart of Your son. You will be able to adjust and correct any of Your illustrious creations.'

"In reply the Universe heard words, in which it recognised the wisdom and majesty of God:

"'My son is the image and likeness of Me. He includes in himself particles of all the diverse energies of the Universe. He is Alpha and Omega. He is creation! He is the realisation of the future! Henceforth and for all time still to come neither I nor anyone else shall be able to change his destiny without his will. All that he wills for himself will be allowed to him. Whatever he conceives, provided it is not conceived in vanity, will turn into reality. My son did not bow before the sight of the maiden's fleshly perfection. Much to the amazement of the whole Universe, he was not amazed by her. Still not consciously aware, My son has sensed all through his feelings. In the first place he sensed that in him something was amiss. And the new creation standing before him — the maiden — did not possess this. My son! My son, through his feelings, senses the whole Universe, he knows everything the Universe possesses.'

"A question filled the whole Universe:

"'What can possibly be missing from one in whom all the diverse energies of ours and Yours exist?'

"And God answered them all:

"'The energy of Love.'

"And the energy of Love flashed with flame:

"'But I am alone, and I am Your very own. I shine by You alone.'

"'Yes! You are alone, My love,' the Divine words proclaimed in reply. 'Your shining light both shines and caresses, My love. You are inspiration. You are able to give everything an acceleration, you accentuate sensations and you are the reconciliation of peace, My love. I beg of you, descend to the Earth in your totality, leaving nothing in its former place. Surround and enfold these My children in yourself, the energy of boundless grace.'

"This farewell dialogue of Love and God heralded the beginning of all earthly love.

"'My God,' Love called out to the Creator. 'When I leave, You will be alone, unseen, for ever, dwelling on all the planes of being. You will be invisible.'

"'May My son and My daughter henceforth shine through the Inner, the Outer and the Order.'[1]

"'My God, around You will be empty space. There will never be a place where the life-giving warmth can penetrate to Your Soul. Without this warmth Your Soul will become cold.'

"'Not for Me alone, but for all life may this warmth emanate from the Earth. My sons and daughters will multiply this radiated Love. And the whole Earth will glow with the warmth of Love shining throughout space. All will feel the light of grace emanating from the Earth, and all My diverse energies will be warmed by its might.'

"'My God, a great variety of paths are exposed to Your son and daughter. In them remain the diverse energies of all the planes of being. And suppose just one of those energies decides to hold sway over the rest, and leads them astray, what can You do, seeing You have thought to give everything away, when You find the energy shining from the Earth start to weaken and fade to naught? You have given everything away, and yet You see how on the Earth the energies of annihilation hold sway over all. Your own illustrious creations are covered with a lifeless crust, and the grass is smothered with stones. What will You do then, what can be done, seeing You have given complete freedom to Your son?'

"'As a green blade of grass I shall be able to break through among the stones anew, and unfold the petals of a flower in a

---

[1] *the Inner, the Outer, the Order* — an approximation of the ancient Slavic terms *Nav', Yav'* and *Prav',* respectively. *Nav* signifies *inner* spiritual reality, the invisible foundation of the *outer,* or visible, material reality (*Yav*), while *Prav* (from a Slavic root word signifying 'right' or 'true') refers to the *order* governing the *Nav* and *Yav* and the relationship between them.

small and untouched glade. My earthly daughters and sons will be able to realise their purpose.'

"'My God, when I leave, You will not be by any eye perceivable. It is conceivable that elements of other energies will begin to speak through people in Your name. Some may try to proclaim themselves rulers over others, abusing Your essence for their own interests, saying: "I speak in God's place, I am His chosen one, everybody listen to me." What will You be able to do in such a case?'

"'I shall come up as the dawn at the inception of the on-coming day. By caressing all creations on the Earth without exception, the rays of the Sun will help My daughters and sons understand that each one in their own soul can hold conversation with My Soul.'

"'My God, many of them will there be, a great sum, and You are alone as one. And all the elements of the Universe will be eager to capture Man's soul. Just to use Man to establish their sway over all through the energy they possess. And Your errant son will suddenly start to pray to them.'

"'There will still be a major obstacle to any attempt, no matter what its form, to lead people awry or lead them into empty space, and this will be a barrier to anything based on a lie. Within all My sons and daughters there is a striving for a conscious awareness of truth. A lie is invariably bound within limits, but truth is unlimited — it will be forever found in the conscious awareness of My sons' and daughters' soul!'

"'O my God! no one and nothing is able to fight or even stand against the flight of Your thought and dreams! They are marvellous! I shall willingly follow them. I shall warm Your children with my radiance and shall perform this service for ever. The inspiration You have given them will help them undertake their own creations. I have only one request to make of You, my God. Allow me to leave just one spark of my love with You.

"'When You are obliged to dwell in darkness, when You are surrounded by nothing but empty space, when oblivion weakens the light from the Earth, then may this spark of my love, even though it seem but a single spark, shine for You with its gleam.'

"O, Vladimir!" Anastasia exclaimed. "If only Man living today could look up to the skies and see what was way above the Earth back then, what a great vision would grace the scene before his eyes! The light of the Universe, the energy of Love, compressed into a comet, hastened toward the Earth, illuminating the still lifeless planets along its course and lighting up the stars above the Earth. Yes, it was indeed heading toward the Earth! Closer, ever closer, it came. And there it was. And all at once, it came to rest over the Earth itself, and the radiance of Love began to resonate. And far away, among the shining stars, one star, smaller than all the rest appeared to be moving. It was hastening to follow the radiance of love on its earthward path. And then Love realised that here was its last little spark from God, and even it was on its way to the Earth.

"'My God!' whispered the radiance of Love. 'But why? I do not understand. But why? You have not left even a single spark for Yourself?'

"To the words of Love, out of the darkness of the Universe, God, already perceivable by no one, gave reply. His Divine words were heard across space:

"'Anything I kept back for Myself would be lacking in My gift to them — My daughters and sons.'

"'My God!'

"'O how marvellous you are, Love, even as a single spark.'

"'My God!'

"'Hasten, My Love, hasten, do not stop for rational contemplation. Hasten with your last spark and warm all My future sons and daughters.'

"The people of the Earth were embraced by the universal energy of Love. All of it, down to the last spark. Everything was there within it where it belonged. Throughout the unfathomable Universe, Man, who lives on all planes of being simultaneously, of all the entities became the most strong."

CHAPTER SEVEN

When Love...

"Adam lay on the grass, among the fragrant flowers. In the shade of a tree he dreamt, as his thoughts churned listlessly along. And all at once a reminiscence swept over him in an unexpected wave of warmth, somehow empowering a strong acceleration of his thoughts. Just recently this new creation stood before me — he reflected — something very much like me, only different, but what is the difference? Where does it lie? And where is this new creation now? Oh, how I wish I could see the new creation once more as I did before! I want to see it again, but why?

"Quickly Adam rose from the ground and looked around. A thought flickered by: What has happened all of a sudden? It is the same sky, the same birds, grass, trees and bushes. Everything is the same, and yet it is different. I am not looking at it the same way as before. The creatures of the Earth, the scents, the air and even the light — everything's become brighter and more resplendent.

"And words were born in Adam's mouth, and he cried out to all: 'And I love in return!'

"And all at once a new wave of warmth came upon him from the direction of the stream, sweeping over his whole body. He turned in the direction the warmth was coming from and, lo and behold, there was the new creation, shining before him. All logic departed from his thought, his whole heart delighted in the vision, when Adam first caught sight of it: there quietly sitting beside a clear pool of water in the stream was the maiden, but after tossing back the braids of her golden hair she was looking not at the clear water but at him. She caressed him with a smile, as though she had been waiting for him a long eternal while.

"He went over to her. As they were looking at each other, Adam thought there could be no one with eyes more resplendent than hers. Aloud he said:

"'You are sitting by the water. The water is good. Would you like to bathe together?'

"'I would.'

"'And then would you like me to show you around... creation?'

"'I would.'

"'I have given everything its designation. I shall command them to serve you too. And would you like me to make a new creation?'

"'I would.'

"They bathed in the stream and ran through the meadow. Oh, how entrancing seemed the maiden's trills of laughter, when after mounting an elephant, Adam conceived a little dance for her and called the maiden's name Eve.

"The day was already drawing to a close as this woman and man stood with all the glory of the Earth around, delighting in its colours, scents and sounds. Quiet and meek, Eve watched the evening descend. The floral petals folded into their buds. The splendid creations of the day faded from sight into the night.

"'Do not feel despondent,' said Adam, by this time already confident in himself. 'It is just that now the darkness of night is coming on. We need it to take our rest, but no matter how much night presses in or how black, the day always comes back.'

"'Will it be the same day, or a new day?' asked Eve.

"'The day will return in whatever form you conceive.'

"'And who is it subject to — each day?'

"'To me.'

"'And who are you subject to?'

"'To no one.'

"'And you, where are you from?'

"'I come from a dream.'

"'And whence comes everything around that is so pleasing to see?'

"'It also appeared from the dream, as a creation for me.'

"'And where is he whose dream is so bright and resplendent?'

"'He is often around, only He cannot be seen with ordinary sight. But all the same it is good to be with Him. *God* He calls Himself, my Father and my Friend. He never offends me, and He gives me everything. I also wish to give to Him, though what — I do not yet know.'

"'That means I too am His creation. Like you, I also wish to show Him my appreciation. To call Him Father, God and Friend. Perhaps we can decide together what actions on our part the Father intends?'

"'I have heard Him say what may bring joy to everyone's heart.'

"'To everyone's? Including His?'

"'Yes, that would mean His too.'

"'Tell me what He desires.'

"'Conjoint creation and joy from its contemplation.'

"'And what may bring joy to everyone on the Earth?'

"'Birth.'

"'Birth? But everything is so beautifully born already.'

"'I often think, before I go to sleep, about an extraordinary and marvellous creation. But with the dawn of the day the dream goes away, and I see that nothing new has come to thought — everything is so fraught with wonder and visible by the light of day.'

"'Let us then think together.'

"'I too wanted, before going to sleep, to be close to you, to hear your breathing, to feel your warmth, to think together about creation.'

"Before going to sleep, impelled by tender feelings for each other, the two embraced in dreams about a marvellous creation, their aspirations connected and merged into one. Their two material bodies reflected the thoughts that had jointly come."

CHAPTER EIGHT

Birth

"The day returned, and night once more came on. One morning, as day was dawning, just as Adam was watching the tiger cubs and reflecting on life, Eve quietly approached him, sat down beside him, took his hand and placed it on her tummy.

"'Feel here, inside me lives my creation — a new creation at the same time. Can you feel it, Adam? Is it pushing, this restless creation of mine?'

"'Yes, I can feel it. It seems to be reaching out to me.'

"'To you? Of course! It is mine, but it is yours too! I very much want to see our co-creation.'

"And Eve gave birth, not in painful labour but in great wonder.

"Forgetting everything around him, not conscious of himself, Adam watched and trembled in anticipation. And Eve bore a new and conjugal creation.

"A tiny wee lump, all wet, lay helplessly on the ground. Its legs were drawn up tight, its eyelids remained closed. Adam watched, his eyes fixed on the little one, as it moved its tiny hand, opened its tiny lips and took its first breath. Adam was afraid to blink lest he miss the tiniest movement. Unfamiliar feelings had begun filling the space within and around him. Unable to restrain himself to the spot, he suddenly leapt up and began to run.

"With no particular destination in mind, Adam rushed headlong along the bank of the stream in great exultation. He stopped. A wondrous, unfamiliar something kept growing and expanding in his chest. And everything around!... The

sound of the wind not only rang through the trees and rus-
tled leaves — it sang, sifting through the rifts of bushes and
setting astir the clusters of floral petals. The clouds not only
swarmed through the sky — all the clouds performed a dance
to entrance the observer as they passed by. The water spar-
kled with a smile as it rushed into the miles of stream before
it. Oh, wow! The stream! Reflecting the clouds the stream
made yet another bend as it gleamed before the eyes. And all
along the birds kept twittering their joyful song in the skies!
And among the herbs the cheerful chirping of crickets could
be heard. And everything fused and blended together into a
single resounding intonation of the tenderest sounds of music known through all God's grand creation!

"After taking a little more air into his lungs, Adam suddenly
cried out as loud as he could. It was not an ordinary cry —
not that of an animal, but one that overflowed with the most
tender sounds. A long sublime hush slowly settled all around.
And for the very first time the Universe heard a Man on the
Earth joyfully burst into song. A Man was singing! And all the
noises that had before sounded throughout the galaxies were
now grounded. A Man was singing! And hearing this happy
song, the whole world of the Universe concluded: not in any
of the galaxies could there be found a single string capable of
producing a better sound than that of the singing of the human soul.

"But the song of rejoicing could not hush Adam's new-
found abundance of feelings. Catching sight of the lion, he
rushed toward it and wrestled it to the ground as though it
were but a pussycat. He laughingly began to run his fingers
adeptly through its mane, then leapt up and, gesturing the
creature to follow suit, ran off across the terrain. The lion
barely managed to keep up with him, while the lioness and
her cubs lagged way behind. Fastest of all ran Adam, his arms
waving, summoning all the creatures to follow in his route.

His creation, he recalled, would be able to bring joy and elation to all.

"And once again he sees the tiny lump in front of him. His own creation! Such a wee little lump — alive! — lapped by the she-wolf and caressed by the warm breeze.

"The baby's eyes had not yet shown a peep — he was asleep. At the sight of him all creatures that had accompanied Adam on his run fell to the Earth in delight.

"'Why yes, it is true!' Adam intoned with exultation. 'Light like my own is emanating from my creation. Maybe it is even stronger than my light, if such an extraordinary thing is happening with me. All creatures have fallen down before it in delight. I desired! I carried through! I created! I created a creation resplendent and alive! All of you! All of you come look at him!'

"Adam cast his glance at all around, and suddenly stopped, his gaze fixed. His eyes were fixed on Eve.

"She was sitting on the grass all alone, caressing with her own lightly fixed gaze the suddenly still and silent Adam.

"And with new might love began shining within and around Adam in invisible delight. And then all at once... Oh, how love universal quivered and shivered to see Adam run up to the resplendent maiden-mother, fall on his knees before Eve, press his hands to her golden braids, her tender lips and her milk-filled breasts. And restraining his exclamation to a gentle purr, he tried to express his exultation in words:

"'Eve! My Eve! My wife! You are able to make dreams come true in life!'

"'Yes, I am woman, your wife. Let us turn into life everything you are able to think of!'

"'Yes! Together! The two of us together! Now it is clear! Two together are we! We are as He! We are able to make dreams come true! Look at us! Our Father, do You hear us?'

"But for the first time Adam could hear no reply. Surprised, he leapt up and cried:

"'Where are You, my Father? Look upon my creation. Perfect and fantastic are all Your earthly creatures. Resplendent are all the clouds, the grass, the bushes and the trees. But my new creation is even finer than the features of the flowers — look at it! I have seen how my own creation has brought me a joy far greater than anything You created through Your dream...

"'You have nothing to say? You do not wish to look at it? But it is by far and away the best part of all! *My* creation, more than any other, is dear to my heart. But what about You? Do you not wish even to look at it?'

"Adam looked at his child. In the spot directly above the tiny sleeping body the air seemed bluer than usual, there was no breeze to ruffle even a hair, only someone was invisibly bending the slender stem of a flower over the baby's lips. And three soft puffs of pollen tenderly touched his lips. The baby smacked his lips, sighed a deep and blissful sigh, moved one of his legs just a tiny bit and then went back to sleep. Adam guessed that while he had been celebrating, God had been cultivating, cherishing the little one, and so had not seen fit to speak.

"And Adam exclaimed:

"'That means You Yourself were helping! That means You were with me all along, and You acknowledged the creation!'

"And he heard in reply the Father's quiet voice:

"'Not so loud, Adam, you'll wake the child with your celebrations and rejoicings.'

"'That means You, my Father, loved both me and my creation? Or did you love it more than me? If so, why? Explain to me! It is not Yours, after all.'

"'Love, My son, has its continuation, and in your new creation will be found your continuation.'

"'That means I am standing here and I am in my creation at the same time? And does that mean Eve is in it, too?'

"'Yes, My son, your co-creation is in all respects like you, only not in the flesh. Within it your spirit and soul merge to give birth to a new creation. And your aspirations will continue and will intensify the joyous sensations multifold.'

"'So, You are saying there will be many of us?'

"'You shall fill the whole Earth. You shall know everything through your feelings, and then in other galaxies your dream will re-create the world anew to be even more resplendent.'

"'Where is the edge of the Universe? What will I do when I come to it? When I myself fill everything, and have created everything I have conceived?'

"'My son. The Universe itself is a thought, a thought from which was born a dream, which is partially visible as matter. When you approach the edge of all creation, your thought will reveal a new beginning and continuation. From obscurity will arise a new and resplendent birth of you, and it will reflect in itself your soul, your dreams, your whole aspirations. My son, you are infinite, you are eternal, within you are your dreams of creation.'

"'Father, it is always so good when You speak. When You are with me, I want to embrace You. But You are invisible. Why?'

"'My son, when My dreams about you were drinking in the diverse energies of the Universe, I did not have time to be thinking about Myself. My dreams and thoughts created only you, they did not make a visible image for Me. But there *are* visible creations of Mine — feel them, but do not try to analyse them. Nobody in the whole Universe will find that they can analyse them simply with their mind.'

"'Father, it feels good to me when You speak. You are with me — everything is with me. If I should find myself at the other end of the Universe, if doubts or crude obscurities should intrude upon my soul, tell me, how might I search You out? Where will You be at such a time?'

"'I shall be in you and with you. Everything is in *you*, My son. You are the master of all the diverse energies of the Universe. I have counterbalanced all the opposite extremities of the Universe in you, thereby making *you* a new creature. Do not allow any of these extremities to hold sway within you. Then shall I be in you alway.'

"'In me?'

"'In you and with you. You and Eve are in your creation. In you there is a particle of Me, and so I am in your creation, too.'

"'I am Your son. What then will be the new creation in relation to You?'

"'Again, it will be *you*.'

"'Whom will You love more — me as I am now, or the me which will be born again and again as before?'

"'Love is one and the same, but there is greater hope in each new embodiment and dream.'

"'Father, how wise You are, I so very much want to embrace You!'

"'Look around you. The visible creations you see are My materialised thoughts and dreams. On the material plane of being you will always be able to communicate with them.'

"'I have loved them, just as I love You, Father. And I have loved Eve, and my new creation too. Love is all around, and I want to be in it eternally.'

"'My son, you shall dwell eternally only in the Space of Love.'

"Years passed, as it were, but time, after all, is a relative concept. Years passed, but why make a list? — for a long time death in himself was something Man could not have even missed. Which means that death, back then, could not even exist."

CHAPTER NINE

The unsatisfying apple

"But Anastasia," I queried, "if everything was so good in the beginning, then what happened afterward? Why are there wars on the Earth today and why are people starving? We have thievery, bandits, suicides, prisons. Too many unhappy families, too many orphans. Where have all our loving Eves disappeared to? Where is God, who promised that we would all live eternally in love? And I just remembered what it says about this in the Bible. God expelled Man from Paradise for picking and tasting the fruit of the forbidden tree. And He even stationed a guard at the gates so as to stop the violators from getting back into Paradise."

"Vladimir, God never expelled Man from Paradise."

"Yes He did, I read about it. He even cursed the Man over this. He told Eve she was a sinner and would bring forth children in sorrow, and Adam would have to earn his living by the sweat of his brow. And that's all come to pass with us today."

"Vladimir, reason it out for yourself, perhaps that kind of logic, or absence of logic, has been devised for somebody's interests, to suit a particular purpose."

"What's logic and somebody's interests got to do with it?"

"Please believe me. Each one must learn to make sense of things, to determine what is true, with his own soul. Only after thinking it through for yourself can you realise that God did not expel Man from Paradise. God remains a loving Father right up to this very moment. He is a God of Love — you must have read about that, too."

"I did indeed."

"So where is the logic then? You will agree that a loving parent would never expel his child from his home. Loving parents, even if it means suffering deprivation themselves, will forgive their children any transgressions they have committed. And God is not indifferent to all the sufferings of people — the sufferings of His children."

"Whether He is or not, I don't know. But one thing everybody knows: He doesn't do anything about them."

"Oh what are you saying, Vladimir?! Of course He will tolerate this distress, too, from His son, Man. But how long can Man go on without a full appreciation of his Father? How long can he go on not seeing or feeling his Love?"

"What you are so concerned about all of a sudden? Be more specific. Where are these manifestations today of the Divine Love for us? Where do we look for them?"

"The next time you are in the city, take a close look around you. The living carpet of marvellous grass has been paved over with lifeless asphalt, all around are harmful masses of concrete called housing, cars scurry around in between them, emitting deadly fumes. But even amidst the stone masses, finding even the tiniest of islands, grass and flowers still sprout forth — God's creations. And through the rustle of leaves and the song of the birds He is still calling out to His daughters and sons to reconsider everything that is happening and to return to Paradise.

"The glow of love emanating from the Earth keeps on getting smaller, and for a long time now the Sun's reflection should have been decreasing, too. But He with His energy is constantly intensifying the life-giving power of even the Sun's rays. Just as before, He loves His daughters and sons. He waits, trusting and dreaming that one day Man will wake at dawn and suddenly regain his conscious awareness, and that this conscious awareness will restore to the Earth its original, pristine blossoming."

"But how did everything on the Earth come to go against God's dreams and for some reason last all these thousands, maybe millions of years? How could He keep waiting and trusting for so long a time?"

"Time does not exist for God. As with any loving parent, He never loses faith. And it is thanks to that faith that all of us are living right now. And we ourselves arrange our lives as we see fit, using the freedom granted us by the Father. But people did not all of a sudden decide to follow the option of a path leading nowhere."

"If not all of a sudden, then how, when? What does it mean, that phrase 'Adam's apple'?"

"Back then, just as now, the Universe was filled with a multitude of living energies. Everywhere there are living elements invisible, the vast majority of them resembling Man's second self. They are almost like people, capable of comprehending all planes of being, but they are not afforded a material embodiment. That is Man's great advantage over them. Furthermore, in the complexes of energies of the Universe's elements one form of energy inevitably holds sway over the rest. And they themselves do not have the capability of changing the proportional relationship among their forms of energy.

"Also, among the elements of the Universe there are complexes of energies similar to God. Similar, yes, but they are not gods. They have momentarily equalised the multitude of energies within themselves, yet, in contrast to God, they are not capable of producing living creations in harmony.

"In the whole Universe nobody has managed to solve the puzzle — the sacred mystery of how or by what power the material plane of being was created, or where the threads tying it and the whole life of the Universe together may be found. Or how or on what basis this plane is capable of reproducing itself.

"When the Earth and everything upon it was created by God, the unparalleled speed of the generative process made it impossible for the elements to understand by what power God was bringing about this grand creation. After everything was already created and was visible, when they noticed that Man was the strongest of all, many were plunged by this resplendent vision first into astonishment, and then into excitement, and finally came the desire to repeat it. To create something similar, all on its own.

"This desire kept on growing. Even today it is still present in a multitude of the diverse energies. They tried to imitate earthly creations in other galaxies, on other worlds, even using the planets which God had created. Many managed to come up with a facsimile of earthly existence, but only a facsimile. The harmony of the Earth and the interrelationship among all things — that is something none have been able to achieve. Thus throughout the Universe, even today, there are planets with life, but this life is but a poor imitation of life on the Earth.

"When all these attempts — not only to produce a better creation but even to repeat the existing one — failed (and God did not reveal His secret), then many of these elements began turning to Man for help. It was clear to them that if Man was God's creation, if Man was God's beloved, then a loving parent could not possibly withhold anything from him. On the contrary, God must have offered great opportunities to Man, His son. And the elements of the Universe started to turn to Man; in fact, they strive to do so even today.

"You know, there are people today who claim that someone invisible is communicating with them from the Universe, calling itself mind and the power of good. Back then, too, right at the beginning, they appealed to Man with requests and exhortations, demanding to know (though hiding their true motives under various guises), by what power the Earth was formed, along with everything existing upon it, and how Man was created to be so great, they wanted to know from what he was fashioned.

"But Man gave an answer to none of them. He did not know the answer to the question himself, nor does he know it today. But he became more and more interested in the question, and began demanding answers from God. Not only did God decline to answer — He tried to inculcate a better understanding in Man, asking him to erase the question from his thinking:

"'I ask you, My son, to create. You have been given the power to create in the space on Earth as well as on other worlds. What you think up in your dream will be turned into reality, you need not doubt. Only one thing do I ask of you: do not try to figure out how, by what power, it all comes about.'"

"What I don't understand, Anastasia, is why God would not want to divulge the specifics of His creation even to Man, His son."

"I can only guess, no more," Anastasia replied. "In not responding to this question even to His son, God might have been trying to protect him from disaster, even deflecting a universal war."

"I don't see any connection between a refusal to respond and universal war."

"If ever the secret of creation were to be revealed, then on other planets in the Universe other forms of life might arise, equal in power to those on the Earth. Two powers might have the desire to test each other. It is possible that such a contest could take place peacefully. It is also possible it could turn out like the wars on the Earth. And that could touch off a war throughout the Universe."

"Indeed," I agreed, "it would be better for the specifics of God's creation to remain a secret. Only one of the elements might happen to figure it out on its own, without hints."

"I do not think any of them would ever figure it out."

"And why are you so confident of that?"

"The nature of the secret is such that it is clear on its own, and at the same time it is not even there, and yet at the same time it is not alone. The term *co-creation* gives me confidence, when I add a second word to it."

"What word?"

"The second word is *inspiration*."

"Well, what of it? What can these two words together signify?"

"They—"

"No, stop! Don't say it! I remember your telling me that thoughts — and that means words too — don't simply disappear into nowhere, they circle around us in space and anyone can catch them. Is that right?"

"Right it is."

"And can the elements catch them too?"

"True."

"Then don't say it. Why give them a hint?"

"Not to worry, Vladimir. Suppose I give them a slight hint as to the secret, I can thereby show them the fruitlessness and senselessness of their constant attempts. That way they can understand and stop bothering Man."

"Well, if that's the case, then tell me, what do *co-creation* and *inspiration* mean?"

"*Co-creation* signifies that in His creating, God used particles of all the diverse energies of the Universe, and His own energy too, and even if all the elements got together to produce a duplicate of the Earth, they would still be missing one particular form of energy — the one that is inherent in God as an idea of His own, the one born in the Divine dream alone. *Inspiration* signifies that the creations were produced through an impulse of inspiration. Who among the great earthly artists and sculptors, after creating their works in an impulse of inspiration, will dare attempt to explain how they held their brush, what they were thinking or where they were standing — these were not the kinds of things they paid attention to, absorbed as they were so completely in their work. Again, there is the energy of Love, which God sent to the Earth. It is free, subject to no one and, preserving its loyalty to God, is in the service of Man alone."

"How fascinating that all is, Anastasia! Do you think the elements will hear it and understand?"

"They shall certainly hear, and possibly understand as well."

"And will they hear what I say, too?"

"True."

"Then I shall sum it up for them. Hey there, elements, is it clear to you now, eh? Don't you go bothering people any more. You'll never guess the Creator's design!... Well, Anastasia, what do you think, did I do a good job of telling it to them?"

"Your final words were quite accurate: 'You will never guess the Creator's design!'"

"Have they been trying to guess it for a long time?"

"Right from the moment they first beheld the Earth and its people, right up to the present day."

"And what harm did their attempts cause Adam, or us for that matter?"

"In Adam and Eve they aroused feelings of pride and self-conceit. And they managed to persuade Adam through a false teaching, saying that to produce something more perfect, it was necessary to break the existing creation down and see what it consisted of, how it worked. They often instructed him to find out how everything was constructed, and then he would be supreme over all. They hoped that when Adam began analysing God's creations to make sense of their construction and purpose, he would comprehend with his mind the interrelationship among the creations of all different kinds. They would then be able to see the thoughts Adam produced and from that they could deduce how they could create like God.

"At first Adam paid no attention to their requests and suggestions. But then one day Eve decided on her own to give Adam some advice:

"'I have heard voices stating things will be even easier and more splendid for us once you ascertain how everything works within. Why should we stubbornly refuse to follow this recommendation? Would it not be better for us to give it a try, at least once?'

"First, Adam broke off a branch of the tree with its marvellous fruit, and then... Then... now you can see for yourself, how Man's creative thought came to a stop, a standstill. Even today he keeps examining things in detail and breaking them apart, trying to analyse the structure of everything and produce his own primitive creations with his thought instantaneously at a standstill."

"Hold on, Anastasia. That's not at all clear to me. Why do you say that human thought has come to a standstill? When people examine something in detail, on the contrary, we say they're learning something new."

"Vladimir, Man is made in such a way that there is nothing he needs to examine in detail. He includes... Oh, how can I make this clearer to you? The structure of everything is included in Man himself, in what you might call an encoded format. The code is deciphered when he tunes into his dream of inspired creativity."

"But I still don't see what harm can there be in taking something apart,[1] and how this can possibly bring thought

___

[1] *taking something apart* — a play on words; the Russian term here (*razborka*) can also signify settling a score between rival gangs.

to a standstill. Maybe it'd be better if you showed me an example."

"Yes, you are right. I shall try an example. Imagine you are at the wheel of your car, driving to some destination. All at once you find yourself wondering how the motor works, and what makes the wheels turn. You stop the car and set about taking apart the motor, for instance."

"So, I'll take it apart, see how it works, and then I'll be able to repair it myself. What's wrong with that?"

"However, while you are taking it apart, your journey is being interrupted. You will not reach your destination on time."

"But I'll still learn more about my car. What's wrong with my acquiring new knowledge?"

"What do you need it for? Your purpose is not to repair, but to enjoy the drive and to create."

"You don't sound very convincing, Anastasia. Not a single driver will agree with you. Except maybe for a few with foreign cars, like Japanese models or Mercedes, which hardly ever break down."

"God's creations not only do not break down, but are capable of re-creating themselves. Hence why should one need to tear them apart to see how they work?"

"What d'you mean, *why?* Just out of curiosity, if for nothing else."

"Forgive me, Vladimir, if my example was unconvincing. If you will allow me, I shall attempt another."

"Go ahead."

"Suppose a beautiful woman is standing in front of you. You feel a burning attraction for her, she appeals to you. And she finds you interesting, too, and seeks to join together with you in creation. But a moment before the mutual impulse for coming together to create, all of a sudden you wonder what this woman is made of. How do her internal organs work?

Her stomach, liver and kidneys? What does she eat and drink?
How will all this function in a moment of intimacy?"

"Enough. Don't go on. You've come up with a jolly good
example there. There will be no closeness, no creation. It
won't work out if this cursed thought comes along. It happened once that way with me. There was one woman I fan-
cied for a long time, but she never gave in to me. And the one
time she agreed, I suddenly thought of how I could perform
better, and for some reason I doubted my ability to perform.
The upshot was that nothing happened. I felt such shame,
and was even afraid I might have lost it for good.

"I later asked a friend about it, and he said the same thing
had happened to him. The two of us even went to see a doctor. The doctor said there was some kind of psychological
factor at work here. There was no use doubting our abilities
or trying to figure out what to do and how. I think this psychological factor causes trouble for a lot of men. Now I get it:
it's all because of those elements, because of Adam, because
of Eve's advice. Yes, they acted pretty bad back then."

"Why are you only blaming Adam and Eve? Look around
you today, Vladimir, is not all mankind continuing to stubbornly repeat the same mistake, violating God's guidelines?
Adam and Eve were not fully aware of the consequences, but
why does mankind stubbornly continue to tear everything
apart? And to destroy living creations? Today?! When the
consequences are so obvious and sad?"

"I don't know. Maybe everybody needs a good shake-up.
Come on, are we so hung up on tearing apart one thing after
another?[2] I just had a thought — maybe it was no use, God
not handing Adam and Eve a decent punishment after all. He
should have given Adam a right good hiding and knocked all

[2] *tearing apart* — again, the Russian term could refer to settling scores by
violence.

that nonsense out of his head — that same nonsense that's causing mankind so much suffering today. And He could have taken a good whip to Eve's soft spot so she wouldn't have gone round getting people into trouble with that tongue of hers."

"Vladimir, God gave Man complete freedom, with no thought of punishment on His part. Besides, punishment will not alter acts committed in one's heart. Wrong actions will continue as long as the original thought is not changed. Tell me, for example, who invented lethal missiles and the nuclear warheads they carry?"

"In Russia it was Academician Korolev[3] who first built rockets like that. But before him Tsiolkovsky[4] theorised about them. American scientists also tried. In any case, a lot of human minds have been involved in rocket design. A lot of inventors in different countries have been working on it."

"Vladimir, there is in fact only one inventor of all rockets and all the lethal weapons attached to them."

"How can there be just one, when whole research centres have been working on rocket design in various countries, and keep their achievements secret from one another? That's what the whole arms race is about: who can produce a weapon best and fastest?"

"This lone inventor takes pleasure in giving out hints to all people that call themselves scientists or inventors, no matter what country they live in."

[3] *Sergei Pavlovich Korolev* (also spelt: *Sergey Korolyov*) (1907–1966) — the Soviet scientist responsible for the design of the first artificial earth satellite — known as *Sputnik* (lit. 'Fellow-traveller') — along with a number of rockets, including the spaceships *Vostok* and *Voskhod,* which carried the first cosmonauts into space.

[4] *Konstantin Eduardovich Tsiolkovsky* (1857–1935) — physicist and mathematician, held to be the father of Soviet space science. He is known, among other things, for his experiments in photosynthesis. He also envisioned human beings colonising other planets in various solar systems.

"And where, in what country, does he himself live and what's his name?"

"*Destructive thinking.* At first it got through to a single individual and took over his material body, producing spears and stone spearheads. Then it proceeded to come up with arrows and iron arrowheads."

"But if it knows everything, this destructive thought, why didn't it go for a missile straight off?"

"The material plane of earthly being does not embody everything thought of all at once. Slowness in matter was given by the Creator to allow people time to think things through. In terms of destructive thinking, the spear, our modern weapons, as well as those of the future, even more deadly, were produced a long time ago. To manifest something more than a spear on the material plane required the construction of a multitude of factories and laboratories that are today termed scientific. Under the guise of plausible excuses more and more people were gradually drawn into the business of turning such deadly thinking into reality."

"And what was the need of constantly trying to do that?"

"To establish itself. To destroy the whole material plane of the Earth. To show to everything in the Universe the superiority of the energies of its all-destructive element over everything else — and, in fact, over God. And it is through people that it acts."

"Sneaky little vermin! And how do we exterminate it from the Earth?"

CHAPTER TEN

Avoid intimate relations with her

"Do not allow it access to your thought or body. All women should avoid intimate relations with men who permit destructive thinking into their consciousness, so as not to reproduce it over and over again."

"Wow! That's quite a thought!" I exclaimed. "If all women gang up like that, all our scientific military minds will go out of their minds."

"Vladimir, if women start acting that way, there will be no war on the Earth."

"Right on, Anastasia! You've struck a blow against all war. Way to go — this idea of yours can wipe out all war! That's quite a blast! It's true — what man would want to go to war if not a single woman would sleep with him after that or bear him offspring — *who?!* That would mean anyone starting a war would be killing himself, his offspring too."

"If women were willing to do this, nobody would ever start a war. Eve's fall from grace would be expiated by women living in today's times, not to mention their own decline, in the face of themselves and God."

"And what will then be occurring on the Earth?"

"The Earth will once again burst forth in its pristine flower."

"You're a powerfully stubborn girl, Anastasia, true to your dream, just as before. But you are also naïve. How can one believe in all the women on the Earth?"

"How can I *not* believe in all women, Vladimir, since I know that the Divine essence is present in every woman living on the Earth today? So let it reveal itself in all its resplendent array! Goddesses! Women of the Divine Earth! Reveal in yourselves your own Divine essence. Show yourselves to the whole Universe in all the beauty of your original pristine presence. You are a perfect creation, you are created from the Divine dream. Each of you is capable of taming the diverse energies of the Universe — dear women, goddesses of all the Universe and the Earth!"

"Now how can you stand there, Anastasia, and state that all the women of the Earth are goddesses? I'm beginning to find your naïvety a trifle ridiculous. Imagine! All of them... goddesses?! Including those standing behind counters, I mean in stores and street kiosks? Cleaning ladies, dishwashers, waitresses? All the ones that cook, bake and wash dishes day after day in their kitchen at home — don't tell me they're goddesses, too?! Sounds like blasphemy to me, even. How can you call drug addicts and prostitutes goddesses?

"Well, now, in a church, okay, or a beautiful lady dancing at a ball — sure, people will say *she's* a goddess. But all those plain types, dressed in everyday rags, nobody's going to call them goddesses."

"Vladimir, it is only a chain of circumstances that makes earthly goddesses spend time in a kitchen day after day. You have stated that I am like some kind of wild creature, that my life is primitive, and that only the world *you* inhabit is civilised. Then tell me why it is that women in your 'civilisation' spend a good part of their life in cramped kitchens? Made to wash floors and carry heavy groceries home from stores? You boast about your 'civilisation', but why is there so much dirt in it? And why do you transform the most beautiful goddesses of the Earth into cleaning ladies?"

"And just where have you seen a cleaning lady who's a goddess? Any women worth their salt shine at beauty pageants and drench themselves to a fault in luxury — and every man wants to marry them. But *they* will only marry men who are rich. As for the plain ones, well, even the poor don't need them."

"Every woman has her own beauty. It is only that not all of them are given the opportunity to reveal this treasure. This great beauty is not something you can measure, like a person's waist, for example. The length of one's leg, the size of one's breasts, the colour of one's eyes — all that is completely irrelevant here. This beauty is interior to the woman, and is found in both a young girl and a woman of senior years."

"Sure, in 'women of senior years'. You're going to tell me about old ladies next! You think they're beautiful goddesses, too?"

"They too are beautiful in their own way. And in spite of the endless humilities they face in everyday life, the multitude of blows dealt them by fate, any woman labelled a 'senior' can still wake up in the morning with the Sun, walk across the dew, smile at the sunrise with a ray of conscious awareness, and then..."

"And what then?"

"And then suddenly make someone love her. She will be loved herself, and she will impart to him the warmth of her love."

"To what 'him'?"

"To the one, her only one, who sees in her the goddess within."

"It doesn't happen like that."

"It does. Go ask some seniors. You will be surprised at how many of them have passionate romances."

"And are you sure that women are capable of changing the world?"

"Capable they are! Capable beyond the shadow of a doubt, Vladimir. Once they change their priorities of love, they — God's perfect creation — will restore to the Earth its resplendent pristine worth, they will transform the whole Earth into the blossoming garden of the Divine dream. They are God's creation! The beautiful goddesses of the Divine Earth!"

CHAPTER ELEVEN

Three prayers

"There you go talking about God, Anastasia, but how do you pray? Or do you pray at all? Many people have requested in their letters that I ask you about this."

"Vladimir, how do you understand the word *pray*?"

"What do you mean, how? Isn't it obvious? *To pray...* that's, well, to pray. Are you telling me you don't understand the meaning of the word?"

"One and the same word can mean different things to different people, depending on how they perceive it. To be able to express myself more understandably, I asked you: What does prayer mean to you?"

"I never really thought about what it means, somehow. Anyway, there's one principal prayer I learnt by heart and sometimes I say it — just, you know, to be on the safe side. Apparently there must be some meaning in it, if so many people say it."

"What are you telling me? You memorised a prayer, and never wanted to find out its meaning?"

"It's not that I didn't want to, it's just I never really thought about its meaning. I thought, well, everybody knows what it means, so why bother thinking? Prayer — well, that's just like having a conversation with God."

"But if this 'principal prayer' signifies a conversation with God, then tell me, how can you talk with God, your Father, without any meaning?"

"I don't know how. What's all the big fuss, anyway, about this *meaning*? No doubt the people who wrote the prayer knew what it meant."

"But would you not like to talk with your Father on your own?"

"Of course. Everybody would like to talk with their Father on their own."

"But how can you talk 'on your own' by repeating someone else's words, especially without even thinking about what lies behind them?"

At first I felt a little irritated at Anastasia's pickiness regarding the meaning of the prayer I had learnt, but then I got interested myself in determining what it meant. For the thought was coming to me all by itself: How did this happen? I had learnt a prayer which I repeated on a number of occasions, but never really thought about what was in the prayer. I thought how interesting it would be to find this out, since I had memorised it. And I said aloud to Anastasia:

"Well, okay, I'll give thought to the meaning at some point."

But she persisted:

"Why 'at some point'? Could you not say your prayer right here and now?"

"Why not? Of course I can."

"Then, Vladimir, say your prayer — the one you term, of all your prayers, the 'principal' one, the one through which you have tried to talk with the Father."

"As a matter of fact, it's the only one I know. And I only learnt *it* because it seems everybody else considers it the most important one."

"All right. Say your prayer, and I shall keep track of your thought."

"Okay. Listen."

I said the Lord's Prayer to Anastasia, which, you may remember, goes like this:

Our Father which art in heaven,
Hallowed be thy name.

Thy kingdom come.
Thy will be done in earth, as it is in heaven.
Give us this day our daily bread.
And forgive us our debts, as we forgive our debtors.
And lead us not into temptation, but deliver us from evil:
For thine is the kingdom, and the power, and the glory
Of the Father and the Son and the Holy Spirit
Always, now and for ever. Amen.[1]

I stopped speaking and looked at Anastasia. But she was sitting there, just as silently, her eyes lowered, not looking at me. She just sat there without a word, with a sad expression on her face, until I couldn't take it any longer and asked her:

"Why aren't you saying anything, Anastasia?"

Without raising her head, she enquired:

"What words are you expecting to hear from me, Vladimir?"

"What d'you mean, 'what words'? I said the prayer without even a single flaw. Did you like it? You could at least say so if you did or not, but you're not saying a word."

"When you were saying the prayer, Vladimir, I tried to follow your thought, your feelings, the meaning of your appeal to God. I understood the meaning of the words of the prayer, but *you* did not understand all the words in it. Your newly budding thought was disintegrating, getting away from you,

[1]Matth. 6: 9–13 (Authorised King James Version), plus two lines translated from an old Russian version of the Lord's Prayer. It should be noted that the Russian text of the prayer includes many obsolete Old Church Slavonic words and expressions that are barely understandable to modern-day Russians (see footnote 2 in Chapter 1 of the present volume: "All this exists right now"). Overall, the frequent use of Old Church Slavonic in the Orthodox Church means that many Russians today associate it with an 'unknown language' (a situation similar to the former predominance of Latin in the Catholic Church).

and there were absolutely no feelings. You were unable to grasp the meaning of many of the words, and you were not addressing yourself to anyone. You were simply muttering."

"But I just said it the way everybody does. I was in church, and there they use even more incomprehensible words. I heard how other people say it. They rattle it off at top speed, and that's it! But I said it to you slowly and distinctly, so you'd understand."

"But before that you said it was a prayer addressed to God."

"Yes, I did say that."

"But God is our Father. He is a person. He is a living entity. The Father is capable of feeling and understanding, when normal communication is initiated. But you..."

"What about me? I'm telling you, that's the way they all say it when they address God."

"Imagine your daughter Polina is standing before you, and all at once she starts talking in a monotone and slips into her sentences words she does not even understand herself. Would you as a father be pleased by her talking to you in such a way?"

I could picture the situation quite clearly, and began to feel downright uncomfortable at the prospect. Here was my daughter standing in front of me, muttering something like a half-crazed person, not knowing what she wanted even.

So I came to a decision: No, I had to make conscious sense of my prayer. I can't just rattle off meaningless words. Otherwise I would appear to God like some half-crazed idiot. If someone wants to mutter it, they can go ahead. As for me, I shall definitely make the effort to understand this whole prayer. I only have to find some place to look up the meaning of unfamiliar words. And why do they speak in some unknown language in church? Aloud I said to Anastasia:

"You know, it's probably not a full and accurate translation. That's why my thought got lost, as you say."

"Vladimir, the meaning can be understood even from this translation. Of course it contains words that are not used any longer in everyday speech. But the sense is clear when you ponder it and decide what is the most important thing of all for you and what is the most pleasing for the Father. What is it you wish to say in uttering this prayerful message addressed to the Father?"

"Well, whatever the words say, that's probably what I want to say, too. I want Him to give me bread to eat, to forgive my sins and debts, to not lead me into temptation and deliver me from evil. It's all clearly set out there."

"Vladimir, God provided food for His sons and daughters even before they were born. Look around you — everything has long ago been provided for you. A loving parent forgives everyone their sins without being asked, and does not even think of leading anyone into temptation. The Father has given each one the capacity to withstand the wiles of evil. Why offend the Father by not realising what He has already provided a long time ago? His eternal gifts are all around you. What more can this loving Parent give, who has already given all to His child?

"And what if there's something missing?"

"God gives to the utmost. He has provided everything for His sons and daughters right from the beginning. Everything! Completely! As a parent who loves His child unconditionally, He can think of no greater good for Himself than the joy which comes from the joyful existence of His children. His own sons and daughters!

"Tell me, Vladimir: How might the Father feel, after giving His children everything right from the beginning and seeing them appear before Him, constantly pleading 'More, more! Keep us, save us, we are all helpless, we are all as nothing'? Please, answer me. Would you as a parent, or any of your friends, wish to have children like that?"

"I can't give you an answer right off. I'll work it out on my own, when I have a quiet moment."

"Yes, yes, of course, fine, Vladimir. Only when you do find the time, think about what the Father would like to hear from you, apart from your requests."

"You mean, God might also want something of us? What?"

"What any parent would wish to hear from his children."

"Tell me, Anastasia, do you yourself ever turn to God in prayer?"

"Yes, I do," came her reply.

"Then tell me your prayer."

"I cannot say my prayer to *you*, Vladimir. My prayer is destined for God."

"All right, talk to God then. I can still hear it."

Anastasia rose, spread out her arms, turned her back to me and began uttering some words. Ordinary words one might hear in a prayer, but... something within me all at once began to tremble. The way she spoke these words was not the way we say prayers. She spoke them the way anyone might talk to a close friend, a loved one, a relative. Her speech contained all the intonations of a live conversation. Passion, joy, fervent ecstasy — as though the One Anastasia was talking to was right there beside her:

My father, You are present everywhere!
For the light of life I gladly thank You,
For Your bright kingdom visible here and now,
And for Your loving will. Long live the good!

For daily bread and daily food with joy I thank You!
And for your loving patience,
And for Your giving of forgiveness of sins on Your Earth fair.
My Father, You are present everywhere!

I am Your daughter here midst Your creations.
Weakness and sin — I shall not let them in,
But prove myself worthy of Your consummations.

My Father, You are present everywhere!
I am Your daughter, Your joy I declare.
My entire self shall magnify Your glory,
In Your bright dream the coming ages all will live and share.
It shall be so! I wish it so! I am a daughter of Yours.
My Father, You are present everywhere.

Anastasia ended her prayer. She continued to communicate with everything around her. It seemed as though she were surrounded by a radiant light. During the prayer, as long as she was near me, something invisible happened all around. And whatever it was touched me too. It wasn't an outward touch, but an inner one. It made me feel good, feel comforted. But as Anastasia drew away, this effect faded, and I called after her:

"You said the prayer as though Someone was standing beside you who could answer it."

Anastasia turned toward me, her face beaming. She spread out her arms, spun around, smiling, and then, giving me a serious look in the eye, said:

"Vladimir, God, our Father, also speaks to everyone with a request, and answers every prayer."

"Then why doesn't anyone understand His words?"

"Words? The peoples of the Earth have so many words with different meanings. There are so many diverse languages and dialects. And yet there is one language for all. One language for all Divine callings. It is woven together out of the rustlings of the leaves, the songs of the birds and the roar of the waves. The Divine language has fragrance and colour. Through this language God responds to each one's request and gives a prayerful response to prayer."

"Could you translate, or express in words, what He says to us?"
"I could give you an approximation."
"Why just an approximation?"
"Because our language is much too poor to be compatible with the language God speaks to us in."
"Never mind, just tell me any way you can."
Anastasia looked at me, stretched her arms out in front of her, and her voice — her voice came forth in chest tones:

My son! My own dear son!
How long I have been waiting. I am still waiting.
A minute holds a hundred years, a moment lasts millennia.
I am waiting.
I have given you all. The Earth is all yours.
You are free in everything. You shall choose your own path.
All that I ask, My son, My own dear son,
Is that you be happy.
You do not see Me.
You do not hear Me.
In your mind are doubts and sorrows.
You are turning away. Whereto?
You are yearning for something. What for?
And you are bowing to someone.
I stretch out my hands to you.
My son, My own dear son,
Be happy, I ask of you.
Again you are going away. But your road leads to nowhere.
On this road the Earth will explode.
You are free in everything, and the world is exploding
And tearing your destiny apart.
You are free in everything, but I shall stand My ground.
I shall restore you to life with the last blade of grass.
And once more the world will shine around.
Only be happy, I ask.

↓   *On the faces of saints a deep sorrow swells.*
You are frightened by judgement and hell.
They tell you that I shall send judges.
But I only pray for that time, as before
When you and I are together once more.
I believe you will return.
I know you will come.
I shall embrace you once more.
Not as a stepfather! Not as a stepfather! I am yours!
I am your Abba, your Father,² the only One,
And you are My very own son, My own dear son,
We shall be happy together as one!

After Anastasia stopped speaking, it took me a while to
recover my composure. Even though it seemed that I was
continuing to listen to all the sounds around me, perhaps I
was really listening to how my blood was rushing through my
veins at an extraordinary tempo. What had I understood? I
cannot understand, even to this day.

Through this fervent interpretation, Anastasia had just set
forth God's prayer to Man. Whether the words were true
or not, who can say? And who can say why they arouse such
strong emotions? And what am I doing at the moment? I
am letting my pen run across the page in conscious excitement — or maybe not so conscious... Am I going out of my
mind? Am I mixing up her words with those the bards now
sing in her name? Anything's possible. Perhaps those that
read this will understand. And I shall try to understand once
I have finished writing. And I am writing again. But again,
just as back there in the forest, as though penetrating a cur-
tain, occasionally lines from those prayers I heard back in the

---

² *Abba, Father* — see Mark 14: 36: "And he [Jesus] said, Abba, Father, all things
are possible unto thee" (Authorised King James Version).

taiga will suddenly appear. And again the question arises — a difficult question, which continues to torment me to this day, through scenes from our lives and ponderings. A question I'm afraid to try to answer, even to myself. But it is not one I can keep back any longer just within myself. Perhaps someone will come up with a convincing answer?!

Prayer! That prayer of Anastasia's! Just words! The words of a taiga recluse, an uneducated recluse, with her own unique way of thinking and her own unique lifestyle. Just words. But for some reason every time I hear them, the veins on my writing hand puff up and the blood pulsates through them more quickly. It pulsates, counting off the seconds in which each of us must decide what is best for ourselves, and how to continue to live. Should we be asking a kind Father to save, give, provide? Or alternatively, confidently and from the heart, suddenly declare, just as she did:

> *My Father, You are present everywhere!*
> *Weakness and sin — I shall not let them in,*
> *I am Your son, Your joy I declare.*
> *My entire self shall magnify Your glory...*

Which prayer will have the most pleasant meaning for Him? What should I do, or what should we all together do? Which way should we go?

> *My Father, You are present everywhere!*
> *Weakness and sin — I shall not let them in...*

But where does one get the courage to speak like that? And to carry it out once the prayer's been said?

CHAPTER TWELVE

Anastasia's line

"Tell me, Anastasia, how did it happen that you and your ancestors lived for so long — millennia, even — in the remote forest, away from society? If, as you say, all mankind is a single body, and all have a single origin, then why is your ancestral line, in contrast to all the rest, a kind of outcast?"

"You are right, we all have One parent. And then there are parents whom we can see. But every human soul has the freedom to chose his own path, leading to a determined goal. Among other things, the choice depends on how one's feelings are nurtured."

"And who then thus nurtured your distant forebears in such a way that your line is so distinctive even today? In your lifestyle, let's say, or the way you understand things?"

"It happened in times long ago. I know I said long ago, but it seems as though it happened only yesterday. Perhaps I can best put it this way: a time came when mankind aspired not to co-creation but to analysing God's creation, back when spears were already flying and hides of faithful creatures were already considered worthy features on people's bodies, when everyone's consciousness was being altered and being directed along the path leading to today, when human thought faltered, aspiring not to creation but to the accumulation of knowledge — all at once people began analysing the process by which men and women were able to experience tremendous satisfaction by merging their bodies together. Then for the first time men began possessing the women, and women submitted to the men not for the sake of co-creation, but so that both of them could experience a satisfying sensation.

"It seemed to them, as it seems to people living today, that such a sensation comes afresh each time there is a merging of the male and female elements, their visible bodies, their flesh.

"In fact the satisfaction from the merging of mere fleshly bodies is fleeting and incomplete. In the intercourse of carnal desire there is no participation by the higher planes of the human self. Man aspired to feel a sense of fulness by changing bodies and methods of coming together, but even today he has not achieved anything fully.

"The sad consequence of these carnal pleasures has been their children. The children were deprived of conscious aspirations toward the goal of realisation of the Divine dream. And women began experiencing pain in childbirth. And the rising generation was doomed to live in torment, and the absence of the three planes of being meant they were afforded no opportunity of attaining happiness in any way. And so we have come down to the present day.

"One of the first women to experience pain in childbirth saw that her newborn baby girl had injured her little leg during the birth and was so frail that she wasn't even able to utter a cry. The woman also saw that the man who had enjoyed sexual pleasure with her remained indifferent to the birth, and was already seeking to pleasure himself with another woman. And so the woman who had chanced to become a mother became annoyed at God. She grabbed her newborn baby girl and ran with it with all her might far away from everyone else, right into the middle of the woods, an isolated place where no one lived. Stopping to catch her breath in her despair, wiping tears from her cheeks, she kept railing at God with words of frustrated anger:

"'Why in Your resplendent world, as You describe it, is there pain, and evil, and repudiation? I do not experience any satisfaction when I turn to look at the world of Your creation. I am in utter dejection and am burning up with anger. I have been rejected by everybody. And the one whom I made love to is now making love to another; he has forgotten about me. And You were the one who made them, see? He is Yours, the one who was untrue and betrayed me. After all, she, the one making love to him, was also made by You. These are your creations, true? And what about me? I just want to strangle them. I am burning up with annoyance at them. Your world has become forlorn and joyless for me. What kind of fate did you select for me? And why did I bear this deformed and half-dead child? I do not want anyone to see it. There is no joy for me in contemplating it.'

"The woman didn't just put the child down — she callously tossed the barely living lump, her own daughter, onto the ground. In her despair and anger she again cried out to God:

"'Let no one ever lay eyes on my daughter! But You look and see. Look and see the torments taking place among Your creations. Her life is not to be. I shall not be able to feed the child that I have borne. My ill temper has burnt the milk in my breast. I am going away. But You look and see! Look and see how many imperfections there are in the world You have created. Let your 'birth' die in Your sight. Let it die among the creations of the Earth.'

"At that the mother ran from her own daughter, angry and forlorn. The newborn baby was left all alone, a barely breathing, helpless little lump, lying on the wooded ground. My distant foremother was in that baby girl, Vladimir.

"God could feel the anger and despair coming from the Earth. He felt distress and compassionate care for that tearful, depressed woman. But the invisible Father who loved her could not alter her destiny. The woman running in despair was wearing a crown of God-bestowed freedom. Every Man fashions the destiny of his own soul. The material plane of being is subject to no one. It is under the complete control of Man himself.

"God is a person. He is the Father of all, but He does not exist in the flesh. Not in the flesh. But in Him there is a complex of all the diverse energies of the Universe, a whole complex of feelings belonging to Man. He can rejoice and He can feel distress, He can grieve over one of His sons or daughters who chooses a path leading to suffering. He glows with a fatherly tenderness to all and each day, for all without exception, He caresses the whole Earth with a sun-ray of love. Day after day He never loses hope that the daughters and sons of His conception will follow the Divine path. Not under orders, not through fear, they will use their freedom of choice to determine their own path to conjoint creation, regeneration and joy from its contemplation. Our Father has faith, and waits. And He sustains life with His Self. Our Father includes the whole complex of human feelings.

"Could anybody imagine how our Father, God, felt, when His newborn child lay quietly dying there alone in His forest wild, among His own creations?

"The baby girl did not cry, she did not even make a sound. The little heartbeat was slowing down. Just occasionally her tiny lips searched around for some life-giving nipple — she felt thirsty.

"God does not have hands of flesh. Even though He is all-seeing, he still could not clasp the baby girl to His breast. Having given everything to Man, what more could He possibly give? And so, He who is capable of filling the whole Universe with the energy of His dream, compressed Himself into a lump of energy over that forest. A wee, tiny lump, capable of dispersing all the vast worlds of the Universe at a single burst. He concentrated the energy of His love right over that forest — the love He expressed toward all His creations. Through them He embodied Himself in His acts upon the Earth. And they...

"And a little drop of rain touched the lips of the baby girl lying there on the ground — lips which were already turning blue — and at once a warm breeze blew. From the trees fell pollen dust, and the baby girl breathed it in. And the day went by, and the night came on, and the baby girl was still alive. All the beasts and creatures of the wild, embraced by a Divine delight, recognised this baby girl as their own child.

"Years passed, the little girl grew and became a young woman. I can call her Lilith.[1]

"As she strode over the ground all bright in the Sun's early rays, all other life around called out her name in gladness and praise. Lilith's smile illuminated and caressed the world God had created around her. Lilith accepted everything around her as we would accept our mother or dad.

"As she grew up, she would venture more and more often toward the edge of the forest. Quietly concealing herself amidst the tall grasses and bushes, she watched as people so similar in appearance to her went about their daily life — but what a strange life it was! They were distancing themselves more and more from God's creations, building houses to live in, cutting down everything around, and for some reason

---

[1]*Lilith* — in Jewish folklore, a female demon of the night associated with owls; in a more recent Hebrew legend, the first wife of Adam in the Genesis story, who refused to subordinate to him and was expelled from Eden to become a malevolent wanderer. However, both the name *Lilith* and her image can be traced back to pre-Jewish traditions. In Sumerian culture the goddess or demoness *Lila* was depicted as a winged woman surrounded by owls. In Sanskrit the term *lila* signifies 'Divine play' and conveys the idea of Creator's enjoyment at the sight of His unfolding creation. In Ancient Gaelic *lili* is a snow-white lily, and the Gaelic feminine name *Lili* to the present day is associated with purity, chastity and innocence. The name of the ancient Slavic goddess of Love — the female aspect of God the Creator — is *Lelia* or *Lilia*, and in ancient Slavic myths a winged goddess in the form of an owl (*Mater' Sva*) is mother of god Svarog, Creator of the Universe. The old Russian verb *lilit'* (in modern form: *leleiat*) means 'cherish' or 'love'.

clothing themselves in animal hides. And they took great pride in killing God's creatures, and boasting about who could most quickly kill their prize. And they kept on producing something out of dead matter. Back then Lilith did not yet realise that people who created dead things out of living things considered themselves thereby to be very wise.

"She aspired to tell these people about things that could bring joy to everyone. She very much desired a conjoint creation and the joy that comes from its contemplation. She felt an ever-growing need within her to bring about the birth of a new, living, Divine creation.

"More and more frequently her gaze rested upon one man in particular. He was rather a plain sort in comparison to his fellows. He did not distinguish himself at spear-throwing, and considered himself a less than successful hunter. He was pensive and often sang quietly to himself. He would often go off on his own and dream about something all alone.

"One day Lilith went out to meet these people. She had collected living gifts from the forest and carried them in a withy basket out to a crowd of people — men standing around a baby elephant they had slain and arguing arcanely about something. And he was there among them, her chosen one. At the sight of her all voices suddenly became mute.

"Now Lilith was a woman of exceptional beauty. She had not taken steps to veil her exposed slender figure, unaware of the hold carnal desires had already secured for themselves over male human beings. They crassly thrust themselves at her en masse. Putting her gifts down on the ground, she noticed the fire of fleshly lust and desire burning in their eyes. And he, her chosen one, ran after all the rest.

"Even from a distance Lilith still felt how forcefully the wave of aggression touched the delicate strings of her soul. Taking a step back, she suddenly turned and ran from the whole approaching horde of warriors.

"Seething with lust, they kept up their chase for a long time. She ran without any difficulty in breathing and did not tire out, while those in pursuit were dripping with sweat. But they were not to lay a hand on Lilith. Those who thirsted to capture this beauty were unaware of the truth that to know beauty, one must include such beauty within one's self.

"And the warriors tired of the chase. Losing sight of Lilith, they started wandering back the way they came and went astray. Eventually they found their way.

"All but one. Weary from running, he sat down on a fallen tree and began to sing. Lilith quietly concealed herself and recognised the singer as the one her heart felt a yen for, who had also given chase after her with the other men in the crowd. Nevertheless she still allowed him to catch sight of her, at a distance, to show him the right way back to his camp. And he followed, but did not run after her.

"Upon arriving at the edge of the forest and seeing his camp and the campfire burning there, he forgot everything and started running toward it. And Lilith watched as her chosen one ran off. Her heart would beat in an unfamiliar way, or all at once stop, as Lilith repeated to herself:

"'Be happy among the others, my beloved, be happy. Oh, how I would love to hear not a sad tune but your gladsome croon here in my forest dear!'

"All at once the runner stopped, and turned back toward the forest, as though pausing in reflection. He looked at the camp and again in the direction of the forest. Suddenly he threw away his spear and confidently took a step forward. He strode over to where Lilith was standing concealed. Lilith kept watching as he walked past her hiding-place, her eyes fixed on him. Perhaps it was her gaze of love that stopped him in his tracks. He turned and walked back in her direction. She did not flee at his approach. She placed her still timid hand onto his outstretched palm. And together they started walking hand in hand, though not a word had yet passed between them. There they were, walking toward the glade where Lilith had grown up — my father the poet, and my foremother.

"Years passed, and the line continued. And in each generation of my forebears, one person at least was inspired by the desire to go visit those other people, so similar in appearance but with quite a different destiny. They would go under various guises. They might mix in with the warriors, or the priests, or pass themselves off as scholars. As poets, they shone with their poetry. They tried to let people know that there was another path to Man's happiness, that the One who created all was right with them, only they need not hide themselves from Him and pursue their vain mercenary interests, or cherish other entities in place of the Father.

"They tried to tell others, and perished. But even when a man or a woman was left alone, through their love they would find a friend among those who lived a different lifestyle, and so our line continued, and with our thinking and our way of life true to our pristine origins, remained unchanged in the end."

Chapter Thirteen

To feel the deeds of all mankind

"Wait, Anastasia," I cried out, after a thought hit me like an electric shock, "you say they all perished. And that that's the way it's been for millennia. And that all the attempts were unsuccessful and all mankind is going its own way?"

"Yes, all the attempts made by my foremothers and forefathers were unsuccessful."

"That means they all perished?"

"All the ones perished that went out among the people and tried to talk to them."

"So that means just one thing — you will perish, too, just like all the rest. You too have started speaking out. And to hope for anything here is just silly. If nobody's ever succeeded in changing the world, or society's way of life, then what makes you think you—"

"Why talk prematurely about death, Vladimir? See, I am still living. And you are here along with me, and our son is growing up."

"But what makes you so confident? What makes you believe that you'll win out where all your forebears failed? All you do is talk, just like they did."

"I just *talk* — is that what you think? At some point you should pay closer attention to the sentences I use. They are not for the intellect. They contain no information which has not been set forth before, but people read them and many experience an emotional stirring within. That is all on account of the way they are constructed so that people can grasp a great deal 'between the lines'. The poetry of their own soul fills in the gaps — whatever is not explicit in the actual text. And now it is not me that is telling them about the Divine truth — the readers are discovering it for themselves. Their numbers are multiplying at an ever-increasing rate, and now there is no diverting them from the path of the dream which belongs only to God. My mission is not yet accomplished, but already the Creator's desire has come true in many hearts. And that is the most important part.

"When the heart aspires to something in a dream, invariably — invariably, believe me, it must all come true in life."

"Then tell me, why wasn't everything set forth in such sentences before this?"

"I do not know. Perhaps the Creator has shone forth with some kind of new energy! An energy that tells us anew about something we see around us every day, something we see but do not pay sufficient heed to or reflect upon. And my feelings do not deceive me — I have the clear feeling that He is accelerating all His diverse energies once more. A new dawn is coming for all the Earth. His earthly daughters and sons will experience life as it was created by the energy of the Divine dream. And both you and I will play our part.

"But most important! Most important are those who have become the first ones to feel those thoughts between the lines, the thoughts that the energy of the Creator has implanted in people, like the music of the soul. It has all happened! It has all come to pass! People are already aspiring to create a new world in their thoughts!"

"You're talking in very general terms, Anastasia. Tell me specifically, what should people do, what kind of world should they build and how, so that everyone in this world can live happily ever after?"

"I cannot tell you more specifically at the moment, Vladimir. Treatises of all kinds are not hard to find in the life of mankind. Many of them have been such that people have fallen down and worshipped them. But none of them makes any sense. Treatises have no power to change the world, and just one point will serve as a confirmation of that."

"What point? I don't understand."

"That point in the Universe designated as a universal limit. The point where all mankind is standing at the moment. And everything depends on the direction in which it takes the next step. All this shows that there is absolutely no sense in tracts. Ever since the beginning of creation the whole of mankind is attracted by feelings alone."

"Hold on a moment, hold on. What about me? Do you mean to say that I have not done everything in my life by virtue of my mind?"

"Vladimir, you, like everyone else, have changed with that mind of yours the interrelationship of material things around you. You have been trying through material means to experience sensations which every Man knows intuitively. Sensations which everyone is seeking but cannot find."

"What kind of sensations? Sensations *everyone* is seeking? What are you getting at?"

"At what people felt back then, in their pristine origins, when they were still living in Paradise."

"So, are you trying to say I've worked to achieve so many things through the power of my mind just so I could discern these feelings of Paradise?"

"But think for yourself, Vladimir, *why* you did all the things you did."

"What d'you mean, *why*? Just like everybody else, I've been making a living for myself and my family. In order to feel that I'm no worse than anyone else."

"'In order *to feel*' — you said."

"Yes, that's what I said."

"Now try to get this through your mind: 'In order to feel'... the deeds of all mankind."

"What d'you mean, *all?* Even the deeds of drug addicts — are they too part of a search for such sensations?"

"Of course. Just like everyone else, they are aspiring to find these sensations, only they are going about it their own way — subjecting their bodies to torture, taking poison in the belief it can help them, just for a moment, experience even an approximation of a great sensation.

"And the drunkard, oblivious to everything, winces and drinks his bitter poison only because the search for a beautiful sensation lives in him too.

"And the scientist harnesses his mind and comes up with some fanciful invention, thinking that this will help him find satisfaction, along with everyone else. But to no avail.

"Over the whole course of its history, Vladimir, human thought has gone and invented a tremendous number of senseless things. Just think of the multitude of objects surrounding you right where you live. And each of those objects is considered to be the achievement of scientific thought. Think of the labours of the multitude of people behind its production. Only please tell me, Vladimir, which of these objects has made you happy and satisfied with life?"

"Which?... Which?... Well, maybe, not a single one, if you look at them individually. But taken all together these objects do a lot toward making life easier.

"Take the motor-car, for example. You get behind the wheel and you can go where you like. It can be cold and raining on the street, but in the car you can turn on the heat. It can be hot and sweaty outside, but inside all you have to do is turn on the air conditioner and you have a nice, cool ride. And in your home, in the kitchen, for example, there's lots of appliances to help women. There are even dishwashing machines to spare the housewife that particular care. And vacuums to clean the rooms through and through and save a lot of time, too. Everyone knows that there's a lot more objects out there like these that can make our lives a lot easier."

"Alas, Vladimir, 'ease-makers' such as these are quite illusory. Man is obliged to pay for them day after day through sufferings and a shortened lifespan. In order to afford these soulless objects, people are obliged to spend their whole life slaving over joyless tasks. The more these soulless objects appear all around us, the more clearly they show the degree of Man's misunderstanding of what constitutes the universal essence of being.

"You are a Man! Take a careful look around you. In order to produce yet another mechanical object, whole factories are built, spewing out deadly pollution, killing the water, and then, you... You, a Man, are obliged to spend your whole life in joyless work for their sake. They do not serve you, but you them, inventing, repairing and bowing down to the things you make. In the meantime, Vladimir, tell me: who among your great scientific minds invented *this* particular mechanism for serving Man, and at what factory was it produced?"

"Which one?"

"The little squirrel with the nut, the one just below my hand."

I looked at Anastasia's hand. She was holding it outstretched, palm face down, about a half metre above the ground. And on the grass, just below her hand, a little red squirrel was standing on its hind paws. In its front paws the squirrel was holding a cedar cone. Its head was first tilted down toward the cone, then perked up high, with its sparkling round eyes fixed on Anastasia's face.

Anastasia smiled, looking down at the little creature. Without a stir she held her hand balanced in the same position as before. And all at once the squirrel put the cone down on the ground, started working on it in some way, using the claws on its front paws to take off the scales and pull a tiny nut out of it. And once more the little creature stood up on its hind paws, raised its head and seemed to be holding the nut out for Anastasia, as though asking her to receive it from its paws. But Anastasia continued to sit on the grass as before, without a stir.

"Then the squirrel lowered its head and quickly bit into the nutshell and, after peeling off the shell, placed the kernel of the nut on a broad leaf. Then it began pulling more and more nuts out of the cedar cone, each time biting into the shell and laying the kernels on the leaf. Anastasia then put her hand down on the grass, palm upturned. Whereupon the squirrel hastily transferred all the shelled kernels from the leaf onto her hand. With her other hand Anastasia gently stroked the furry little creature, which had become stock still. Then it came even closer to Anastasia and stood, apparently trembling with joy before her, and looked her in the eye.

"Thank you!" Anastasia said aloud to the squirrel. "Today, my beauty, you are better than ever before. Go on, go about your business, my busy little one. Find your chosen one, my beauty, one who is worthy." And she motioned with her hand toward a nearby cedar tree with huge, spreading boughs. Whereupon the squirrel began skipping about, twice executing a circle around Anastasia before bounding off in the direction indicated by her arm. With a flying leap onto the trunk, she finally disappeared into the cedar's leafy branches. In the meantime, on Anastasia's hand, now stretched out toward me, lay the neatly shelled cedar nut kernels.

Well now, that's quite a mechanism, I thought to myself. It collects the product, delivers it, even separates it from the shell. This little creature doesn't require any maintenance or repair, and doesn't consume any electrical energy.

After trying the nuts, I asked:

"What about the great military leaders — Alexander the Great, Julius Cæsar, the ones who started wars, Hitler too —

don't tell me they were searching for a feeling of their pristine origins?"

"Of course they were. They wanted to feel that they were rulers of the whole Earth. Subconsciously they felt that this kind of sensation was related to the one everybody is intuitively searching for. But they were mistaken."

"Mistaken, you say. What makes you think that? After all, nobody has yet been able to take control of the world."

"But they took control of cities and whole countries. They would fight and win battles over cities, but the satisfaction they derived from their victory was fleeting indeed. And they kept on warring, aspiring to even greater conquests. Their invasion of a country, almost inevitably more than one, would bring them no relief but only more grief. And the fear of losing everything. And once again they tried seeking satisfaction through military deeds. Their minds were so immersed in vanity that they could no longer count on them to bring them to the dream of the great Divine sensations. All the military leaders of the Earth met with a sad end. And the whole history of the world, insofar as we know it today, bears this out. Unfortunately, however, the vanity, the ramblings and the parade of mercenary dogmas do not allow people living today to discern where exactly the Divine sensation awaits them along the way."

CHAPTER FOURTEEN

Dining in the taiga

Each time I visited Anastasia in the taiga, I would invariably take along things to eat. I would take preserves, hermetically sealed biscuits in a plastic wrap and sliced fish fillet in a vacuum pack. And each time when I got ready for the trip back, I would find my reserve supplies unused. And each time she would slip some treats into my backpack. These generally consisted of nuts, fresh berries wrapped in leaves, and dried mushrooms.

Russians are accustomed to eating mushrooms — well boiled, fried, marinated or salted. Anastasia eats them in their dried, natural state, without any processing. At first I was afraid to even try them — then I tried them, and they were okay. Once a piece of mushroom is softened from the saliva in the mouth, you can suck on it like candy or swallow it. Later I even got so I liked it.

One time I was travelling from Moscow to Gelendzhik by car for a readers' conference. The whole trip I lived on mushrooms Anastasia had given me. Alexander Solntsev,[1] the director of the Moscow Anastasia Centre, was at the wheel and he ate some of the mushrooms, too. And during my talk at the conference I invited the audience to try them, and people didn't shy away. They kept taking one piece each until my supply ran out, and ate it on the spot, and nothing bad happened to any of them.

[1] *Alexander Solntsev* — see footnote 4 in Book 2, Chapter 25: "The Space of Love".

In fact, I don't remember any occasion during my visits with Anastasia where we actually sat down for the specific purpose of eating. Whatever Anastasia offered me, I would just try on the spot, and I never felt any real sensation of hunger. But this once...

At the time I was probably too engrossed in pondering the meaning of Anastasia's prayer to notice how she managed to spread such a huge table, if, indeed, one can call it that.

There on the grass, on a variety of leaves both large and small, lay a host of delicacies. They filled an area larger than a square metre in size. And everything was beautifully laid out with tasteful decor — cranberries, huckleberries, cloudberries, raspberries, black and red currants, dried strawberries, dried mushrooms, some kind of yellowish paste, three small cucumbers and two medium-sized red tomatoes. These lay among a multitude of clumps of herbs, decorated with floral petals. Some sort of white liquid, looking not unlike milk, stood in a little hollowed-out wooden bowl. I couldn't tell what the scones were made of. There was honey in the comb, too, strewn with multicoloured grains of pollen dust.

"Seat yourself down, Vladimir, try this God-given daily bread," Anastasia invited, with that sly smile of hers.

"Wow!" I couldn't restrain myself from exclaiming. "That's really something! And you've laid it all out so beautifully! Just like a good mistress of a feast."

Anastasia bubbled with child-like joy at my praise. Then she burst out in laughter, her eyes still fixed on the 'table' she had laid out. All at once she threw up her hands in the air and exclaimed:

"Oh-oh! You see, here I am supposed to be a good feast-mistress and yet I have gone and forgotten my spices. You like a lot of hot spices, do you not? You like them, yes?"

"I do."

"And here this 'good feast-mistress' has gone and forgotten them. Give me just a moment. I shall correct my mistake."

She took a look around her, ran off a little ways and tore off part of a herb, then did the same in another place. Then she reached into the bushes and tore off something else, and presently laid her find down amongst the cucumbers and tomatoes — a little bouquet-like clump of various herbs. Then she explained:

"These are spices. They are hot. Try them if you like. Now we have everything. Take a taste of everything, Vladimir."

I picked up a cucumber, surveyed the variety of taiga foods spread out before me and said:

"Pity there's no bread."

"Bread there is," Anastasia responded. "Look here." And she handed me some kind of tuber. "This is a burdock root. I prepared it specially so you would find it a replacement for tasty bread and potatoes and carrots."

"I never heard of burdock being used for food."

"Try it. Not to worry — in times past people used it to make a great many tasty and healthful dishes. Try just a small bite first. I have been keeping it in milk, to soften it."

I was about to ask where she got the milk, but once I took a bite of the cucumber... I couldn't say another word until I had finished it off — and without bread yet. I took the bread-replacement tuber from Anastasia, but I could only hold it in my hand without trying it until I had finished eating the cucumber.

You see, this ordinary-looking cucumber was utterly different in taste from any I had ever eaten before. This taiga cucumber had a pleasant unique fragrance. You're no doubt aware that cucumbers grown in hothouses taste quite different from those raised in garden beds in the open air. The ones growing in the open have a significantly superior taste and fragrance. But Anastasia's cucumber surpassed all the open-air cucumbers I had tasted before, and possibly by an even greater margin of difference.

I quickly picked up a tomato, tried it and polished it off on the spot. Its taste, too, was extraordinarily delicious. Like the cucumber, it was far tastier than any other tomato I had ever eaten. Neither of them required any salt, sour cream or salad oil. They were delicious in and of themselves. Just like a raspberry, or an apple or an orange. Nobody would ever think of either sweetening or salting an apple or a pear.

"Where did you get these vegetables, Anastasia? Did you run down to the village? What kind are they?"

"I grew them myself. You liked them, did you not?" she asked.

"Like them?!! I've never had any like these before! That means you've got a garden plot, or a hothouse? What kind of tools do you use to dig your beds? Where do you get fertiliser — at the village?"

"The only thing I got at the village was some seeds from a woman I know there. I prepared a spot to plant them among the herbs, and they grew. The tomatoes I planted in the autumn, then hid them under the snow, and come springtime they began growing. The cucumbers I planted in the spring, and they — those little ones — managed to ripen."

"But what makes them so delicious? Is it some new variety?"

"Just an ordinary variety. They are different from those grown in a typical garden plot only because they were provided with everything they needed during their growth period. In garden-plot conditions, when people try to isolate their plants from contact with other species and accelerate their growth by using fertiliser, the plants are unable to take in everything they need to become self-sufficient and please Man."

"And where do you get your milk? How do you make your scones? I thought you didn't use any kind of food from animals, and yet here you've got milk..."

"That milk is not from animals, Vladimir. The milk you see before you is from a cedar."

"How d'you mean, from a cedar? Can a tree actually give milk?"

"It can. Only not all trees, by any means. But cedars, for example, can. Try it — there is so much included in this drink. The cedar milk before you can nourish more than just your body. Do not drink it all at once — try one or two sips, otherwise it will fill you up so much that you will not want anything else."

I took three sips. The milk was thick, with a pleasant, slightly sweet taste to it. I also felt a warmth from it, but not the same as from warmed cow's milk. This tender, inexplicable warmth ran through my whole insides and, I think, changed my mood at the same time.

"This cedar milk is delicious, Anastasia. Delicious indeed! But how does one 'milk' a cedar, to get this liquid?"

"There is no 'milking' involved. You must keep grinding the milk kernels of the nut with a special stick in a wooden mortar — calmly, thoughtfully, with a good attitude. And you keep adding water — little by little — living spring water... and you end up with the milk."

"Are you saying people have never known about this before?"

"Many people knew about it in times past, though even today people in the little taiga villages sometimes drink cedar milk. People in cities prefer a different kind of diet altogether — one less healthful but more suitable for the purposes of conserving, transporting and cooking."

"What you say is quite correct. When you live in a city you have to do everything quickly. But this milk... Wow! What kind of tree is this cedar?! The cedar all by itself can give us nuts and oil, and flour for scones... and milk!"

"And there are lot of other unusual things that the cedar can supply."

"What unusual things, for example?"

"You can make superb perfume from its ether oil. Self-sufficient, healthful perfume. Nothing artificial can come even close to its fragrance. The ethers of the cedar represent the spirit of the Universe. They can cure the body — the ethers of the cedar can protect Man from harmful influences."

"Can you tell me how to extract perfume like that from the cedar?"

"I can, of course, but now you, Vladimir, should have a little more to eat."

I reached out my hand to take another tomato, but Anastasia stopped me.

"Wait, Vladimir, not that."

"How d'you mean?"

"I prepared a variety of things for you, so that you could first take a taste of everything, so that it might cure you."

"What might cure me?"

"Your own body. Once you try a bit of everything, the body itself selects what it needs. You will feel like eating more of what you have chosen. Your body itself will determine what it needs."

Wow! — I thought — *for the first time she's gone against her own principles.*

What happened was that twice before Anastasia had cured me of some internal ailments. What kind of ailments, exactly, I don't know, but I used to get bad pains in my stomach, or my liver, or my kidneys. Or maybe all of them at once. The pains were bad, and painkillers didn't always help. But I knew that when I came to see Anastasia, she would cure me — something she does very quickly.

But on the third occasion she refused to treat me. She didn't even completely remove the pain with her gaze, saying that if I wasn't going to change my lifestyle or eliminate what was causing me to be ill, there was no point in treating me, since in that case the treatment would only harm me. I got really angry at her and never asked her for treatment again.

After returning home, I did find myself cutting back a little on the amount of smoking and drinking I indulged in. I even fasted for several days, and felt better. And then the thought came: we don't have to go to a doctor or some other healer every time we feel ill — we can take hold of our own selves when we feel pain pressing down upon us. Of course it would be best for it to not press down at all. I wasn't able to cure myself completely, but I decided not to ask Anastasia for help. However, she agreed to treat me, all on her own.

"But you did say you wouldn't give me any more treatment or even take away the pain."

"I shall not take away your pain any longer. Pain is a conversation between God and Man. But, I can now... since I am just offering you food — that does not go against Nature, although it does go against *them*."

"Who's *them*?"

"The ones who thought up the régime that is so harmful to Man."

"What harmful régime? What are you getting at?"

"At the fact that you, Vladimir, like the majority of people, feed yourself according to an established dietary régime. A very harmful régime."

"I guess some people follow a kind of régime. There are lots of diets out there — for losing weight, or for gaining weight. But I eat what I want. I never read up on *any* régime. I go into a store and I pick out what I like."

"That is right: you go into a store and choose, but your choice is restricted to what is offered by the store."

"Well, yes. In stores today everything's neatly pre-packaged. Because of the tremendous competition, all the producers nowadays try to please the consumer, and do everything for the consumer's convenience."

"Do you think it is all done for the consumer's convenience?"

"Sure — for who else?"

"All systems under a technocratic way of living invariably
work only for themselves, Vladimir. Do you consider it 'con-
venient' to get those lifeless frozen or tinned foods, or water
that is half-dead? Was it your body that determined the selection of foodstuffs available in grocery stores and supermarkets?

"The technocratic world's system has taken upon itself the
role of supplying you with the necessities of life. You have
agreed to this, you have complete faith in it, to the point that
you have even ceased to wonder whether you *have* been sup-
plied with all the necessities."

"But we're still alive — we aren't dying from using these
stores!"

"Of course you are still alive. But the pain! Where do you
think your pain comes from? Think about where pain comes
from with the majority of people. Disease and pain are not
natural for Man, they are the effect of choosing the wrong
path in life. Now you will be persuaded of that for yourself.
Here before you lies just a small sampling of what the Divine
Nature has created for Man. Just try a little bit of each thing,
and then take what you like with you. Three days is sufficient
for these little herbs — which you yourself will select — to
overcome your pains."

I began trying a little of everything while Anastasia was still
speaking. Some of the clumps of herbs were tasteless, while
others I felt like eating more of. Before my departure Anastasia put the things I had taken a liking to into my backpack.
I ate them over a three-day period. And the pain completely
disappeared.

CHAPTER FIFTEEN

They're capable of changing the world?

"Why is it, Anastasia, that every time you speak of your forebears, you always talk about mothers, about women? As for men, your forefathers, I hardly hear anything. It's as though the fathers in your line were all insignificant. Or maybe your genetic code, or your Ray, doesn't allow you to feel your male ancestors? Isn't that a bit insulting toward your forefathers?"

"I can feel and see the deeds of my forefathers, just as I can my foremothers, when I want to. But I am far from being able to *understand* all their deeds, or to determine their significance for the present day — for me and everyone else."

"Tell me at least about one of your forefathers whose deeds you don't fully comprehend. As a woman, you find it harder to understand men. It'll be easier for me, seeing I'm a man. If I understand, then I can help you understand, too."

"Yes, yes, of course, I shall tell you about my forefather who was able not only to discern but also to produce living substances of a power greater than all the weapons known, either today or in the future. Nothing manufactured could ever withstand them — they are capable of changing the earthly world, of destroying galaxies or even creating whole new worlds."

"You must be joking! And where is this gadget today?"

"Any Man living on the Earth today is capable of producing it provided he can understand, and can feel... My forefather revealed part of the mystery to the Egyptian priests. Even today, earthly rulers in their political states govern according to the system and mechanism established by those priests. But now there is less and less understanding of the meaning and the mechanism of government. This mechanism was not perfected, and has become degraded over the centuries."

"Hold on, hold on a minute, there. You're saying that today's presidents rule their countries according to a system or directions worked out by the priests of ancient Egypt?"

"Since that time, Vladimir, nobody has ever contributed anything significant of their own to the system of government. And today's earthly states have no conscious awareness of how the government of human society works."

"Now that's simply too hard to believe. Can you try taking me through the whole thing step by step?"

"I shall try taking you through it all step by step, and you try to understand.

"Tens of thousands of years ago, before the world witnessed the grandeur of Egypt, when no state like that yet existed, human society was divided into a multitude of tribes. My forefather and foremother's family lived apart from human society, they lived according to their own laws. They were surrounded in their glade by everything as it was back in their pristine origins, as in Paradise. My foremother, a beauty herself, had two Suns — one of them was the orb of day, which, as it rose into the sky, awakened everything to life. The other was her chosen one.

"She was always up first. She bathed in the stream and warmed herself in the rising Sun. The light of joy was something she always shared with everything around, and she waited. She waited for *him* to awaken, her loved one. As he awoke, she caught his first glance. When their glances met, it was as though everything around them fell into a trance. Love and trembling, comfort and ecstasy were excitedly taken in by the Space around them.

"The day passed by in joyful duties. And each time the Sun began sinking toward sunset, my forefather always watched thoughtfully, and then he sang.

"My foremother listened to his singing with hidden ecstasy in her heart. Back then she did not yet understand how the words interwoven into the song were forming a new image, an extraordinary image. More and more often she felt like hearing about it, and as though feeling my foremother's desire, my forefather sang about it again and again, and each time he sang he outlined the unusual features more and more distinctly. The invisible image came to dwell among them.

"One morning upon awakening my forefather did not encounter the glance of love that he usually did. He was not surprised. He quietly rose and headed into the forest. In a secluded spot he caught sight of my foremother, enfolded in silence.

"She was standing there all by herself, leaning against a cedar tree. Enfolded in silence, she felt my forefather put his hands on her shoulders. She kept her moist eyes lowered, instead of raising them to look at him. He lightly touched a tear running down her cheek, and said tenderly to her:

"'I know. You are thinking about *it*, my beloved. You are thinking about it, and you are not to blame for that. The image I created is invisible. It is invisible, but you love it more than you love me. You are not to blame for that, my beloved. I am going away. I am going now, out among the people. I have been able to discern how splendid images are created. I shall tell the people about that. What I know, others can know, too. And the splendid images will lead people into the pristine garden. There is nothing more powerful in the Universe than the substance of living images. The image I created has proved itself even stronger than your love for me. Now I shall be able to create grand images. And these images will serve people.'

"My foremother's shoulders trembled, and a trembling voice whispered:

"'But why? You, my beloved, have created an image which I love. It is invisible. But you who are visible are going to be leaving me. Our child is already stirring within me. What shall I tell him about his father?'

"'The splendid images will create a splendid world. Our son will picture to himself, as he grows, the image of his father. If I am able to become worthy of the image pictured by my son, then my son will recognise me. If I am not worthy of his conception, I shall stay on the sidelines, so as not to interfere with his aspiration to the dream, the splendid dream.'

"Incomprehensibly to my foremother, my forefather went away. He came to the people. He came with a grand discovery enthralled. He came for the sake of his future sons and daughters, in an aspiration to create a splendid world for all."

Chapter Sixteen

An extraordinary power

"It transpired in those days that the tribes of people living on the Earth engaged in frequent frays. And every tribe planned to raise as many warriors as it could. And among the warriors any that aspired to the culture of the land or the culture of poetry were looked down upon. And each tribe had its priests, who essayed to make the people afraid. But none of them had any clear goal; they simply found solace in others' fear. And each one flattered his own pride by telling himself he was receiving from God more of something than his fellows.

"My forefather managed to assemble a group of poets and priests from a number of different tribes. There were nineteen in all: eleven poet-singers, seven priests and my forefather. They got together in a deserted, isolated spot.

"The singers sat with meek faces to one side, while the priests took their places with a show of pride. My forefather addressed them as follows:

"'The tribes can be made to cease their enmity and war. And all the peoples will then come to live in a single state. They will have a single just ruler, and every family will be saved from the horrors of war. People will start to offer each other help. And the brotherhood of people will find their way to the garden of their pristine origins.'"

"At first the priests simply laughed at my forefather, telling him he was daft:

"'Who will voluntarily surrender his power and authority to another? If all tribes are to come together, one of them must become the strongest and overcome the others, and here you conceive of there being no more war. Your words are too naïve to ponder. Why have you gathered us together, you slow-witted wanderer?!' And the priests began to leave. But my forefather stopped them by saying:

"'You are wise men, and your wisdom is needed to make laws for human society. I can give each one of you such power that no weapon made by human hand can withstand it. If you cherish it and use it for a good trust, it will help everyone reach their goal, come to the truth, to a bright sunrise that is blissful and grand. But if its possessor lusts in his soul to fight others with an evil intent, he himself will perish.'

"This reference to extraordinary power arrested those priests in their tracks. Whereupon the high priest proposed to my forefather:

"'If you know of such an extraordinary power, tell us about it. And if this power actually works, and is capable of creating whole states, you will stay and live with us in that state. Together we shall create laws for human society.'

"'This was precisely why I came to see you: to tell you about this extraordinary power,' my forefather replied to all. 'But first I would ask you to nominate a ruler from among all those known to you. A ruler who is kind, whose mind is free from greed, who lives with his family in love and, as to war, has not a single thought thereof.'

"The high priest mentioned to my forefather in reply that there was indeed a ruler who studiously avoided all contentions. But his tribe was small in terms of numbers, and since there was no tendency to glorify its warriors, this was something few among them aspired to become. And so to avoid conflicts, they were often required to change their base and move on, abandon a place that was more suitable for living and settle in a less favourable space. This ruler's name was Egypt.

"'Then Egypt shall this state be called!' my forefather said. "I shall now sing you three songs. You, my dear poet-singers, shall sing these songs to people in all the different tribes. And you, my dear priests, shall settle yourselves among the people of Egypt. Families from all over will be drawn to you, and you shall greet them with good laws.'

"Whereupon my forefather sang three songs to those gathered. In the first song he formed the image of a just ruler, calling him Egypt. The second song conveyed the image of a happy people living together in harmony. In the third song was the image of a loving family with happy children, fathers and mothers, residing in this extraordinary state.

"The songs were made up of ordinary words already familiar to everyone. But the words were combined in such a way as to cause their listeners to hang on each new combination with bated breath. And then there was the captivating melody in the resonant voice of my forefather. It beckoned and called, fascinated and created living images.

"At that time there was still no outward Egyptian state, its temples had not yet been built, but my forefather could tell that it would all come about as a result of the calling of Man's thought and dream, melding into one. And my forefather was enthralling in his song, inspired by the extraordinary power with which our grand Creator has endued us all. He sang as one who possessed this power — a power that distinguishes Man from everything else, that gives Man dominion over all, that allows Man to be recognised not only as the son of God but as a creator too.

"Now fervent with inspiration of their own, the poet-singers sang these three songs amongst the various tribes. The people were fascinated by the splendid images created, and came from all over to dwell with the tribe of Egypt.

"Just five years later, out of this very small tribe, the state of Egypt was born. All the other tribes which had earlier vaunted themselves above their neighbours simply fell apart. And there was nothing the war-inclined rulers could do to stop it.

Their authority weakened, and disappeared completely. They were defeated by something, but there was no war.

"Accustomed to material conflicts, they had no idea of the power the images held over all — images that delighted people's souls and fascinated their hearts.

"In the face of but a single image, provided it is genuine and untainted by mercenary interests, all the armed troops of the Earth are useless, whether they carry spears or any other deadly weapons. Before this image all warriors fall to the ground, powerless.

"The Egyptian state grew and increased in strength. Its ruler was dubbed *pharaoh* by the priests. Ensconced in their temples away from the everyday bustle of mankind, they made laws, which even the ruling pharaoh was obliged to follow. And every ordinary citizen was only too glad to carry them out. And each one aspired to live his life in conformity with the image.

"My forefather lived among the high priests in the main temple. And for nineteen years the priests paid heed to him. They aspired to study the supreme science of all sciences, to learn how to create grand images. My forefather was inspired with the best of intentions and sincerely endeavoured to explain everything to them. Whether they understood it fully or only in part is no longer clear, and it does not really matter all that much.

"Then one day after nineteen years, the high priest called a meeting of his inner circle of priests. They filed into the main temple with solemn dignity — a temple which even the pharaoh was not allowed to enter.

"The high priest took his place on the throne, while all the rest sat at his feet. My father smiled as he sat there among those priests. He was immersed deeply in thought, composing yet another song, either creating a new image, or perhaps rejuvenating an old one.

"The high priest addressed the gathering as follows:

"'We have learnt a grand science indeed — one that allows us to rule all the world, but in order to perpetuate our reign, we must ensure that not one grain of it goes beyond these walls. Now we must create our own tongue and communicate exclusively in it amongst ourselves, lest any of us let something slip, even by chance.

"'Over the ages we shall circulate among the people a multitude of treatises, at which everyone may marvel, and think that it has all been set forth. And we shall set forth a multitude of marvellous sciences and various discoveries in such a way that both the rulers and the common people will move further and further away from what is important. And so that wise men in the centuries to come may amaze others with their sagacious treatises and sciences. Moving further and further away from what is important themselves, they will lead others in the same direction.'

"'So be it!' they all agreed with the high priest. With the exception of my forefather, who alone remained silent.

"And the high priest continued:

"'There is one question requiring our urgent attention. Over the past nineteen years we have learnt how images are created. Any one of us is now capable of creating an image that can change the world, destroy or strengthen a state — and yet the secret of the power itself has never been revealed. Can any of you tell me why the images each of us creates vary in power? And, in terms of time, why does it take us so long?'

"The priests were silent. None of them knew the answer. The high priest went on, ever so slightly raising his voice, and his sceptre trembled ever so slightly in his hand as he told those assembled:

"'In the meantime there is in our midst one who is capable of creating images very rapidly, and the power of these images remains unsurpassed. For nineteen years now he has

been teaching us, but there remains much that he has yet to
tell. Now we must realise that we are not all equal among
ourselves. It matters not who holds what rank among us. But
everyone should know that there is one among us who holds
the power to control in concealment, unseen, in his sway.
With power of the images he is capable of creating, he can
elevate or slay. One among us is capable of deciding the fate
of nation-states. I as high priest am empowered to alter the
balance of power. The doors of the temple wherein we sit are
closed. A loyal guard stands outside the door and will open it
to no one except on my command.'

"The high priest rose from his throne and with heavy steps,
striking his sceptre against the stone slabs of the floor, headed
toward my forefather. In the middle of the hall he suddenly
halted and addressed my forefather:

"'Now you shall choose one of two paths. Here is the first.
You shall now reveal before us all what you have concealed:
the secret behind the power of your images. You shall tell us
how and by what means they are created, and then you shall
be proclaimed a priest second only to me, and upon my departure you shall become first. All living people will bow before you.

"'But if you do not reveal your secret to us, a second path
will be yours. It leads only to that door.'

"Whereupon the high priest pointed to the door leading
out of the temple hall into the tower, in which there were no
windows nor supplementary exterior doors. This high tower
with smooth walls did have an exterior platform up above,
from where on an appointed day once a year my forefather or
some other priest would sing to an assembled crowd.

"Still pointing to the tower door, the high priest added:

"'You shall go in through that door and never come out of
it. I shall command the door to be walled up, leaving only a
small opening through which you will receive a daily minimum

of food. When the time comes for people to gather by the tower, you shall go out to greet them from the platform up above. You shall go out, only you shall not sing nor create any images. You shall go out so that the crowd will see you and not become concerned or spread rumours surrounding your disappearance. You shall be allowed to greet the people with words only. If you should dare sing a song to create images, even a single song, you shall be deprived of food and water three days long. For two songs you shall not receive food or water six days long, which means you will be decreeing your own death. Now decide and tell us clearly which of these two paths you have chosen.'

"My forefather now calmly rose from his place. His face betrayed neither fear nor rebuke, only a sense of sorrow lay gently on his furrowed brow. As he made his way past the priests sitting in his row, he looked each one of them in the eye. And in each pair of eyes he beheld the thirst for knowledge. But not only the thirst for knowledge: greed itself glared at him from each pair of eyes. Then my forefather went up close to the high priest and stared him in the eye. The grey-haired high priest in turn did not take his eyes off my forefather — eyes which likewise burned with greed. Striking his sceptre against the stone floor, he sternly repeated to my forefather's face, saliva foaming in his mouth:

"'Hurry up and decide, which of the two paths is your choice.'

"My forefather's voice betrayed no fear as he calmly replied:

"'Perhaps it is the will of fate, but I choose a path and a half.'

"'How can you choose a path and a half?' exclaimed the high priest. 'Do you aim to make fun of me, and of all those who are currently in the Great Temple?!'

"My forefather went over to the tower door, then turned and replied to all:

"'Believe me, I would not even think of making fun of you or offending you. At your will I shall enter into the tower for good. But before I go I shall reveal to you the secret as best I can, and I know that it is not my reply that will bring me the second path. That is how it turns out that my choice is a path and a half.'

"'So tell us! Do not halt or waste time!' The voices of the priests leaping up from their seats rang even stronger through the vaulted arches of the Great Hall. 'Where is the answer to the secret? Keep it from us no longer!' they begged.

"'It is in an egg,' my father calmly replied.

"'In an egg?!! What egg? What are you talking about? Out with it!' The assembled priests kept plying my forefather with questions, and he responded:

"'A hen's egg will bring forth a hen's chicken. A duck's egg will give birth to a duckling. An eagle's egg will bring an eagle into the world. Whatever you feel yourselves to be, that is what you will bring forth.'

"'I feel! I am a creator!' the high priest all at once professed. 'Tell us how to create the image that is stronger than all the rest.'

"'That is not the truth,' my forefather replied. 'You yourself do not believe what you are saying.'

"'How can you know what power of faith I have?'

"'One who creates will never bring himself to entreat. One who creates is capable of giving of himself. You, on the other hand, are one who entreats, which means you are already well within the shell of unbelief.'

"My forefather went through the door, which at once shut behind him. Later, following the high priest's order, the entrance was walled up. Once a day my forefather was handed food through a small opening. The rations were meagre, and he was not always given enough water.

"As the day approached when the throngs of people were to gather before the tower to hear new tales and songs, for three days my forefather was allowed no food, only water. That was on the order of the high priest — a change from his original decree. He gave this new order so that my forefather would become weak and not be able to sing any new creative songs to the crowd.

"When the multitude of people gathered in front of the tower, my forefather went out to greet them from the platform up above. He gave the waiting throng a cheerful look. As to what had happened to him he breathed not a word. He simply sang. His voice rang forth in a song of rejoicing, and an extraordinary image was born. The people who had gathered to hear him paid close attention. Directly he finished his song he began a new one.

"The singer stood and sang from his high platform the whole day long. As the day drew to a close, he announced to the whole throng: 'With the new dawn you will hear new songs.' And on the following day he sang again. The people were unaware that the singer, imprisoned as he was in the tower, was no longer being given even water by the priests."

Listening to Anastasia's account of her distant forefather, I wanted to hear at least one of the songs he sang, and I asked:

"Anastasia, if you can reproduce in such detail like that all the scenes from the life of your forebears, couldn't you sing a song too? The song your forefather sang to the people from the tower."

"I can hear all these songs myself, but a full and accurate translation of them is impossible. Many of the words simply do not exist in today's language. And many of the words used back then have a different meaning now. Not only that, but it is difficult to reproduce the poetic rhythms of that time in the word-combinations we have today."

"Pity. I very much wanted to hear those songs."

"You shall hear them, Vladimir. They will rise again."

"What d'you mean, they'll *rise again*? You just said a translation is impossible."

"A full and accurate translation, yes, is impossible. But it is possible to create new songs in the same spirit and with the same meaning. Bards are creating them right now, using words familiar to everyone today. The final song my forefather sang back then you have already heard."

"Heard? Where did I hear it? When?"

"A bard from Yegorevsk[1] sent it to you."

"He sent me a lot of songs."

"Yes, he did, but one of them is very similar to my forefather's final song."

"But how could that have happened?"

"Times have their own continuity, Vladimir."

"So what kind of a song is it, what words does it contain?"

"You will understand in just a moment. I shall explain everything in order."

---

[1] *Yegorevsk* (pron. *yi-GOR-yivsk*) — an industrial town about 100 kilometres south-east of Moscow, founded by decree of Empress Catherine the Great in 1778. The site of the new city had previously been known as *Vysokoe* (lit. 'High'), dating back to 1328; on a number of occasions through the centuries Vysokoe had won special favour from the reigning Tsar and his family.

Chapter Seventeen

When fathers will understand...

"On the third day my forefather once more climbed up to the platform with the dawn. He stood there smiling, looking at the throng of people. He was looking for someone specific in the crowd. Itinerant singers waved at him in greeting and raised their instruments, and their strings vibrated under the singers' inspired hands. My forefather kept smiling at them while at the same time he scanned the crowd even more carefully. My forefather wanted to see his son. To see the son born to his loved one nineteen years earlier in the forest. Suddenly out of the crowd he heard a resounding young voice:

"'Tell me, O great poet and master of the song. You are standing up there, high above everyone. I am down here, but why do you seem so close to me, as though you were my father?'

"And their dialogue was heard by all around.

"'Why young man, do you not know your own father?' enquired the singer from the platform up above.

"'I am nineteen years old, and I have not seen my father even once. I live with my mother alone in the forest. My father left us before I was born.'

"'First tell me, young man, how do you see the world around you?'

"'The world is splendid with its rosy dawn and the setting Sun drawing the day to a close. Marvellous and multifaceted it is. But people are crassly perverting the beauty of the Earth, and causing each other to suffer.'

"From the high tower came the voice in reply:

"'Perhaps your father left you because he was ashamed before you, ashamed of the world into which he brought you. Your father left, aiming to make the world a more splendid place for you.'

"'And so, did my father believe that he would be able to make over the world all by himself?'

"'The day will come when all fathers will understand that they are the ones given the responsibility for the world in which their children live. The day will come when every father will face the fact that before bringing his beloved child into the world, he must act to make the world a happier place. And you as well must give thought to the world in which your own offspring will live. Tell me, young man, how soon is your chosen girl to give birth to the one which she has conceived?'

"'In the forest where I live I have no chosen girl. The world there is splendid, I have a host of friends. But I still have not yet met a girl who is willing to go with me into my world — a world I cannot leave.'

"'Well, then, even if you have not yet seen your chosen girl so fine, you still have a space of time to make the world into at least a little more joyful place for your future girl or boy.'

"'I shall devote myself to that, just like my father.'

"'You are no longer a growing lad. You have flowing within you the blood of a fine young man, a future poet and master of the song. Sing to the throng about your splendid world. Come, you and I together shall join in song. We shall sing along together of the splendid world of the future.'

"'Who can sing when your own voice is so resounding, O poet and master of the song?'

"'I tell you, young man, you shall be able to sing that way as well. I shall sing the first line, the second is your verse. Only sing out boldly, as I have told you, my poet.'

"My forefather sang from the high tower. Over the heads of the assembled throng the voice soared forth with rejoicing, and out came the line:

I arise, and the dawn smiles, befriending...

"And from the throng standing below, all at once a pure and resonant voice, not yet self-confident, carried on:

I walk miles, and the birds sing above...

"And after each line of the father's came that of the son, and sometimes their voices blended as one, and a resonant song of joy resounded all around:

And this day will have never an ending,
Because ever more deeply I love.

"At that point the young man found his confidence and with rank ecstasy sang on:

Along the Sun's road with light footsteps a-stealing,
I enter my Father's own ground,
My eyes see the path, but my feet have no feeling,
My happiness now knows no bounds.
I remember my seeing this all once beforetime:
The flowers, the trees and the sky.
Back then I could see only pain and misfortune,
But now, You are everywhere nigh.
It's all still the same — the bright stars and the birdies,
But I look at them differently now.
I have no more sorrow, I feel no more hurtings,
I love all you people — oh, wow!

"The voice from the tower grew fainter and fainter, and before long it could not be heard at all. The singer in the tower momentarily lost his balance, but quickly regained it, and smiled at the people once more. And right up to the end he noticed how his son's voice was ever stronger than before. The voice of his son, now master of the song, standing below in the throng.

"When the song was ended, my forefather, from his position on the tower platform, waved farewell to the throng. To conceal himself from human eyes, he descended five steps on the staircase inside the tower from the platform doorway. He was becoming weaker and losing consciousness, but he perked up his hearing to the limit. From the wind he could just catch the words fervently whispered to the young singer by a young and beautiful girl:

"'Allow me, young man, allow me... I shall follow you, I shall go with you into your splendid world...'

"There on the stone steps of the walled-up tower my forefather was fast losing consciousness. He had a smile on his face as he awaited death. With his last breath his lips whispered:

"'The line will continue. You will find bliss in a circle of happy children, my beloved.'

"My foremother heard him in her heart. Over the thousands of years to come poet after poet would repeat the words of the song of my two forefathers. And the words and phrases of that song were reborn all by themselves among poets of various times and lands. They have sounded forth in many tongues. These simple words conveyed truth, and they broke through artifice and dogma. And now once again they are heard today. Whoever deciphers their lines — not with the mind but with the heart — will learn great wisdom."

"And was there some sort of special meaning in the other songs your forefather sang from the tower?" I asked. "Why would he give his life just for some songs?"

"My forefather, Vladimir, created many images in his songs. They later built a state and maintained it for a long time. It was these songs that helped the priests — the descendants of those first priests — to create a multitude of religions, and take power in different lands. But there was just one thing the priests did not know, when they decided to use their power for selfish ends. The priests did not know how to make the images work for them in perpetuity. The images lost their power when the priests tried to subject them to their own selfish pride. The ones —"

"Hold on, hold on there, Anastasia. There's something I fail to understand about the images."

"Forgive me, Vladimir, for my lack of clarity. Now I shall try to let go, pull myself together, and tell you, all in its proper order, about the most important of all sciences. The *science of imagery*, it is called. All our ancient and modern sciences are derived from it. The priests split it up into parts so as to conceal the most important thing, in an effort to maintain their power over everything on the Earth in perpetuity, passing on their knowledge of it to their descendants in underground temples by word of mouth. And they tried to preserve the secret with such zeal that their modern-day priest descendants have been afforded only a tiny fraction of that science. But back then, when it all began, things were going considerably better for the priesthood."

"And just how did it all begin? Tell me everything right from the start."

"Yes! Yes, of course. I somehow got excited once more. I must tell you everything in order. The conscious awareness of this powerful science began with the songs resounding forth from the tower."

Chapter Eighteen

He celebrated the joy of life

"When my forefather sang from the high tower, images were born from his songs. The throng standing below included singers and musicians. And all the priests of the time took their places with solemn dignity amidst the multitude. The priests feared most of all that some image exposing and incriminating them might be born in those songs, that my forefather might recall how the priests imprisoned him in the tower. But from his position on the platform high on the walled-up tower the singer sang only songs of joy. He painted a picture of a righteous ruler, with whom the people could live happily ever after. And he offered an image of wise priests. And he depicted the country and the people living in it as fruitful and prosperous. No one was exposed or incriminated, but in his songs the joy of life was celebrated.

"The priests, who for the past nineteen years had been studying the science of imagery, probably realised more than the rest what the singer was doing. They kept watching people's faces and saw how their eyes lit up with inspiration. They watched how the poets' lips moved and the musicians quietly fingered the strings of their instruments in time with the singer.

"My forefather had been singing from the high tower for two whole days. The priests calculated in their minds for how many thousand years this one person, standing there in front of everyone, was creating the future. At dawn on the third day the words of the final song rang out, which my forefather sang with his son, and when he made his final exit, the throng of people listening to them broke up and began heading for their homes.

"The high priest remained at his place for a long time. As he thoughtfully sat there, the priests standing silently about him noticed how his hair and even his eyebrows were turning white right before their very eyes. Then he arose and ordered the entrance to the tower to be re-opened. And the entrance to the tower was opened once more.

"There on the stone floor was the poet's body lying lifeless. Only two metres or so separated his weakened hand from a piece of bread. Between his hand and that piece of bread a wee little mouse ran back and forth, squeaking. The wee little mouse kept begging and waiting for the poet to take his bread and share it with the creature, but the mouse itself would not touch the bread. It was waiting and hoping for the singer to revive. Upon catching sight of the people coming in, the wee little mouse jumped back toward the wall, but then ran over to the feet of the people silently standing around. The wee little mouse's two little beady eyes tried to look these people in the eye. The priests standing on the grey stone slabs of the floor took no notice of it. Then it hastily ran over to the piece of bread once more. The wee little grey mouse squeaked desperately, and even dragged the piece of bread over to the lifeless body of the singer, poet and philosopher, trying to push it into his hand.

"The priests buried my forefather's body with high honours in an underground temple. But they made it so nobody would take notice of his grave under the stone slab floor. And bending his grey head over my forefather's grave, the high priest said:

"'None of us will ever say of himself that he understood how he could create great images as you did. But you are not dead. We have but buried your body. The images you created will live on for thousands of years around and above the Earth, and you are in them. Our descendants will make contact with them in their souls. Perhaps someone in some future age will be capable of learning the essence of creation, of learning what people need to become. And we must create a great and splendid doctrine, and keep it for thousands of years out of sight, until one or the other of us or our descendants discovers to what Man should consecrate his great and splendid might."

CHAPTER NINETEEN

A secret science

"The priests created a secret science. Their doctrine was known as the science of imagery, and from it all other sciences have been derived. To keep the secret, the high priests divided up the whole science of imagery, and caused the other priests to think in differing directions. Hence astronomy, and mathematics, and physics came along quite a bit later, as well as a multitude of other sciences, including the occult sciences. They were all developed for the simple purpose of drawing people's attention to individual sectors, thereby ensuring that nobody would ever be able to break through to the core of the teaching."

"But what kind of core are you talking about? What kind of science is it, and what does it consist of — this 'science of imagery' that you speak of?"

"It is a science that allows Man to accelerate his thought and think in terms of images, to grasp the whole of the Universe at once and penetrate a microcosm, to create invisible yet still living substance-images and use them to control a large community of people. Through the help of this science a multitude of religions came about. One who had even the slightest knowledge of it possessed incredible power, and was able to conquer countries, and topple kings from their thrones."

"And does that mean that a single individual could take over a country?"

"Yes, that is right. And the procedure involved is very simple."

"Is even one fact like this known to today's historians?"

"It is."

"Tell me about it. I don't remember anything like that myself."

"Why waste time in telling about it? If you go back and read about Rama, or Krishna, or Moses, you will see their creations — the creations of priests who had learnt a part of the secret science of imagery."

"Well all right then, I shall read about their deeds, but how shall I arrive at the essence of this science? Try telling me yourself about its essence — what did they learn about it and how?"

"They learnt to think in terms of images, as I told you."

"Yes, you told me, only it's still not clear to me what connection mathematics, say, or physics, has with this science."

"One who masters this science does not need to write out formulas, or outline or create a variety of models. He is able to penetrate matter mentally, right down to the nucleus, and split an atom. But this is just a simple exercise to learn how to control people's destinies and those of the populations of various countries."

"Wow! I've never read anything like that."

"But what about the Bible? There is an example in the Old Testament when the priests were competing amongst themselves to see who could create the strongest images. Moses the priest against the pharaoh's high priests. Moses cast his rod down in the sight of everyone and turned it into a serpent. And the priests of the pharaoh's court did the same thing. Then the serpent created by Moses swallowed up the other serpents."[1]

"You mean to say all that actually happened?!"

"Yes."

[1]See Exodus 7: 8–12.

"I thought somebody just made it up, or it was a kind of metaphor..."

"Nothing made up, Vladimir. It all happened just the way the competition is described in the Old Testament."

"But what made them compete in front of each other that way?"

"It was to show who could create the strongest images, capable of conquering other images. And Moses proved to everyone that he was the strongest. After that it was senseless to fight against him. Instead of fighting they were obliged to carry out his requests. But the pharaoh did not listen, he tried to stop the Israelites from following Moses' leadership and the image he created. But the warriors were not strong enough to stop the people of Israel — a people in which a more powerful image resided.

"Then you can read about how the people of Israel many times conquered other tribes, and took their cities. About how the people created their own religion and nation-state. The glory of the pharaohs lost its shine. But at the time when the priests of Egypt still excelled in their creation of grand images, when they were able to determine what consequences an image they created would provoke among the people, Egypt flourished under the control of the priests. Of all the known states formed after the last global disaster, Egypt flourished the longest."

"No, wait a moment, Anastasia. Everybody knows that Egypt was ruled by the pharaohs. Their pyramid tombs have lasted right to the present day."

"Outwardly, the executive power in the country *did* rest with the pharaohs. But their chief task was to exemplify the image of a wise ruler. The important decisions were not taken by the pharaoh. Whenever the pharaohs tried to seize full power for themselves, the state would start deteriorating at once. Each pharaoh was, first and foremost, appointed to the

throne by the priests. The pharaoh himself studied with the
priests from very early childhood, and endeavoured to master the science of images. Only by learning its fundamentals
could he hope to be appointed a pharaoh.

"The power structure prevalent at that time in Egypt can
today be described as follows. At the very top were the secret
priests, then the priests who looked after educational and judi-
cial matters. Control of the state formally rested in the hands
of a council of representatives of all the priestly ranks, while
the pharaoh ruled according to their laws and did as he was told
by them. The community leaders had a good deal of executive
power — they were considered more or less independent.

"In fact, things were pretty much the same as they are today. Many nation-states have a president and government as
their executive authority. Parliament, like the priests of old,
makes the laws. The only difference is that today there is no
provision in any country for the president to be instructed as
the pharaoh was instructed by the priests. The same applies
to those who hold public office today on councils, Dumas[2]
or congresses. It does not really matter by what term today's
legislator-priests are called; what matters is that they too have
nowhere to turn to learn how to become lawmakers before
they actually take on the job. How can our lawmakers learn
wisdom when the science of imagery is kept secret? That is
why we have chaos in many nation-states."

"What are you trying to say, Anastasia? If we modelled
our governments on the power structure that was in place
in ancient Egypt, everything would have turned out for the
better?"

"The actual power structure can bring about very little in
the way of change. It is much more important what stands behind it. And when it comes to the Egyptian power structure,

[2]*Duma* — the name of the Russian parliament.

Egypt was not ruled by it, nor by the pharaohs, nor even by the priests."

"Then by whom?"

"In ancient Egypt everything was ruled by images. Both the priests and the pharaoh subjected themselves to them. From the ancient science of imagery a secret council composed of just a few priests took the image of the pharaoh as a just ruler. They took the image just as it appeared at that time. This secret council spent a good deal of time discussing the proper conduct for a pharaoh, his outward trappings and lifestyle. Then they taught one of the selected priests how to exemplify this image.

"They tried first to select a candidate from the ranks of royalty. But if no one of royal blood was found suitable in appearance or character, they could choose any priest and pass him off as pharaoh. The priest selected as pharaoh was always obliged to conform to the conceived image, especially during public appearances. And then each member of the public felt the invisible image hanging over him and acted according to his understanding of it. When people believe in an image and the majority find it to their liking, each one is only too happy to follow it, and the state has no need to set up a huge official surveillance apparatus. Such a state can only grow stronger and flourish."

"But if that were so, then no state today could get by without images. And yet they do get by, they are alive and flourishing. Just look at America, or Germany. And our own Soviet Union, before *perestroika*,[3] was a tremendous state."

"Without an image, Vladimir, no state can get by even today. Today it is only the state in which the governing image is

[3]*perestroika* — the policy of restructuring the economic and political system of the Soviet Union, which led to the collapse of the Communist Party's hold on power and to the break-up of the USSR.

the most acceptable to the majority of people that flourishes, compared to other states."

"Then who is creating this image today? After all, there are no priests around any more — at least not the kind ancient Egypt had."

"There are still such priests today, only they are called by another name, and have within them less and less of the science of imagery. Today's priests are not able to make impartial and long-term calculations. Not able to set a goal and create a worthy image capable of drawing the whole country to that goal."

"What are you talking about, Anastasia — what kind of priests, or images, were there in our Soviet Union? Everything back then was controlled by the Bolsheviks.[4] First Lenin, then Stalin was in charge. Then came other First Secretaries.[5] They had the Politburo.[6] Religion was pretty much eliminated back then, they even destroyed the temples — and here you go carrying on about priests!"

"Vladimir, take a closer look. What was there before the state which came to be known as the Soviet Union emerged?"

"What d'you mean, what was there? Everybody knows. It was the tsarist régime. Then along came the revolution, and we went down the path of socialism, at the same time trying to build communism."[7]

"But before the revolution actually took place, the image of a new and just system of governance with a bright outlook

---

[4]*Bolsheviks* — the majority party at the time of the Russian Revolution in 1917. The term is derived from the Russian word signifying 'majority'.

[5]*First Secretaries* — Under the Soviet system, the First Secretary of the Communist Party was the *de facto* leader of the country.

[6]*Politburo* (a term derived from the Russian words signifying 'political bureau') — the chief policy-making committee of the Communist Party, responsible to the First Secretary.

was already circulating among the people, and the old system was being exposed. After all, initially it was the image of a new state that was being formed, along with the image of a new ruler who would be most benevolent to everyone. And the image of everyone leading a happy life. It was images such as these that led people on and motivated them to fight against those who were still loyal to the old images. And both the revolution and the civil war[8] which followed it — a war which involved multitudes of people — were in fact a conflict between two competing images."

"Of course there might well be something in what you say," I admitted. "Only Lenin and Stalin weren't images. Everybody knows they were merely human beings who happened to be leaders of their country."

"You bring up these names, thinking that behind them stood simply people in the flesh. In fact... Perhaps if you think about it, you will see that it was very far from being that way, Vladimir."

"How could it not be that way? I'm telling you: everybody knows that Stalin was a Man."

"Then tell me, Vladimir, what sort of Man was Stalin?"

"What sort? The sort... Well, in the beginning, everybody thought him to be kind and just. Someone who loved children. There were photos and portraits of him holding a little girl in his arms. Thousands of soldiers went into battle crying 'For the Motherland! For Stalin!' Everyone wept when he

---

[7]*socialism/communism* — In official Communist Party pronouncements, the political status quo in the Soviet Union was designated 'socialism', while the country was in the process of 'building communism' — i.e., working toward the goal of becoming a truly communist state.

[8]civil war (*grazhdanskaya voina*) — In Russia this lasted from the 1917 Revolution up to 1922, when the Bolsheviks (or 'Reds') finally consolidated their power, defeating the 'White' forces loyal to the Tsar.

died. My mother used to tell me that when he died practically the whole country wept. And they placed him in the Mausoleum[9] next to Lenin."

"So, that means that a great many people loved him and triumphed in deadly conflicts with their enemies in his name? They dedicated poems to him, but what do they say about him today?"

"Today they say he was a bloodthirsty tyrant and a murderer. He let multitudes of people rot in prisons. They unceremoniously removed his body from the Mausoleum and buried it in the ground, and destroyed all the monuments to him, along with the books he once wrote..."

"Now do you understand? You see before you two different images. Two images, but the same Man."

"The same."

"So what kind of Man was he — can you tell me now?"

"I guess I can't... Can you tell me anything yourself?"

"Stalin as a Man corresponded to neither of these two images — before or after — and therein lay the tragedy for the nation. There has always been tragedy in states where a significant discrepancy has come up between the ruler and his image. That is where all national troubles have begun. And in these times of trouble people have fought for the images with the gun. It is only recently that people were still attracted to the image of communism, but the image of communism has deteriorated, and now what are you and everybody else in the nation attracted to?"

"Now we are building... well, capitalism, maybe, or maybe something else, but just so that we can live the way they do in the developed countries — like America, or Germany, for

---

[9] *Mausoleum* — a large marble structure on Red Square just outside the walls of the Kremlin, where visitors can still see the embalmed body of Lenin.

instance. Anyway, so that we can have democracy, like they have over there, and an abundance of everything."

"Now you are identifying the image of your country and a just ruler with the image of those other countries you name."

"Okay, let's say it's the image of those countries."

"But is that not admitting that the knowledge of the priests in your own country has completely diminished? There is no knowledge left? They have no more power to create a worthy image capable of leading people in its path? As a rule, any state in such a situation has been a dying state, as thousands of years of history attest."

"But what's wrong with our starting to live the way they do, say, in America, or Germany?"

"Take a closer look at how many problems there are in the countries you name. Ask yourself why they need such huge police forces and great numbers of hospitals. And why are there more and more suicides there? And where do people from the rich big cities go for their holidays? And they constantly require increasingly greater numbers of officials to watch over the public. All this means that their images are deteriorating, too."

"And what is the result — that we are attracted to their deteriorating images?"

"Yes, the result is that we are thereby prolonging their life, but not by much. When they destroyed the leading images in your country, they did not create any new image in its place. And everyone was allured by an image that was prevalent in a foreign country. If they all keep bowing down to it, then your country will cease to exist — it is a country which is losing its own image."

"But who is able to create such an image today? We don't have any Egyptian-style priests."

"There are people even today who are wholly involved in creating images and determining the ability of images to attract a nation's people, and their calculations are frequently quite accurate."

"For some reason I've never heard of such people. Or is it all top secret?"

"You, like a great many people, come into contact with what they do on a daily basis."

"Oh, where? When?"

"Vladimir, remember, when the time comes to elect new deputies to the Duma,[10] or to select a single ruler out of several candidates — he's called a *president* today — how their image is presented to the people. And those images are put together by people who have chosen image-making as their profession. Each candidate has several such people working for him. And the winner is the one whose image is the most favourable to the majority of voters."

"What d'you mean, 'image'? These are all real live people. They get up on the hustings in front of voters and even go on TV themselves."

"Of course, they appear themselves, only they always get advised as to where they should go, how they should behave, what they should say, so as to fit the image most favourable to the people. And, more often than not, the candidates heed this advice. In addition, a variety of advertisements are made up for them, attempting to associate their image with a better life for all."

"Yes, they do advertise. All the same, I don't really know what's more important — the Man himself who wants to become a deputy or president, or the image you keep talking about."

"Of course the Man is always more important, but when you vote for him, after all, you probably have not had the

---

[10] *deputies* — Members of the *Duma*, or Russian parliament, are known as 'deputies' (*deputaty*).

opportunity to meet with him, you do not know in detail what he is actually like — you are voting for the image which has been served up to you."

"But each candidate still has a platform, and people vote for the platform."

"How often are those platforms carried out once the candidate is elected?"

"Well, not all pre-election platforms are carried out by any means, and maybe none of them ever gets fully carried out, because other people with their platforms of their own get in the way."

"So each time it turns out that a multitude of images is created, but there is no complete unity among them. There is no single image capable of attracting everyone and leading them to a goal. If there is no image, then there is no inspiration, and no clear path. Life becomes *ad hoc* and chaotic."

"Then who is capable of creating such an image? Priests of wisdom, we've seen — there simply aren't any today. And as for the science of imagery which your forefather taught the priests of old, well, I'm learning about that for the first time from you."

"There is not much longer to wait — the country *shall* have a strong image. It will end all wars, and people's dreams in splendid clarity will start coming into birth — first in your country, and then all over the Earth."

CHAPTER TWENTY

Our genetic code

Anastasia spoke with absorbed interest. Sometimes joyfully, sometimes dejectedly, she spoke about what happened on the Earth at one time. Some things were believable, others not so much. And when I got home I wanted to find out about people's ability to hold in their memory information about events going back not just to their own birth but to the birth of their ancestors, and even further back, to the creation of the first Man. Scientists and specialists on this subject got together on a number of occasions, and here I should like to offer a few pertinent excerpts from the round tables we had.

"...To many people it will seem strange to claim that everyday objects can contain information about a Man. But if you show an audiocassette to someone who's never seen a tape recorder or even heard about its possibilities, and tell him that your voice, your speech, is recorded on the tape and he can listen to it whenever he likes — a year or even ten years later, that person will not believe you. He'll think you're some kind of trickster. Yet for us the fact of recording and reproduction of sound is a common occurrence. And by the same token something that seems quite extraordinary to us might be extremely simple and natural to someone else."

"If we start from the fact that Man has still not invented anything more substantial or perfect than what has been invented by Nature, then Anastasia's ray, which helps her see things at a distance, can be confirmed by the existence of the radiotelephone and television. Further, I would say that those phenomena of Nature which she uses sound like a more perfect application than what we have invented artificially, like our modern television and radiotelephone."

"One person's memory may have a hard time keeping track of things that occurred even half a year ago. Another person may remember events that happened in his childhood and be able to talk about them. But I don't see that as coming anywhere close to the limits of the human memory's possibilities."

"I don't think many scientists will deny that Man's genetic code has been storing primordial information for millions of years. It is also possible to collect supplementary, so-called 'incidental' information over one's lifetime and pass it on to succeeding generations. Expressions we are all familiar with — like "it's inherited" or "transmitted by inheritance" — bear witness to this. Anastasia's abilities to reproduce scenes that happened to mankind millions or billions of years ago are theoretically possible and explainable. Not only that, but they can be at their most accurate the further they are removed from our reality. I believe Anastasia's memory is not that different from many other people's. Or to put it more accurately, the information recorded in her genetic code is no greater than for any other individual. The only difference is that she has the ability to 'retrieve' and reproduce it fully, while we can do so only in part."

These and other things the specialists said have convinced me that Anastasia is able to tell the truth about the past. I was especially struck by the example of the tape recorder.

But there was one phenomenon which the scientists invited to the round table couldn't explain — namely, how it is that Anastasia can get information not only about earthly civilisations but also about those on other worlds and in other galaxies. Besides, she can not only talk about them, but it seems she can also influence them. I shall try to set forth everything in order. Perhaps someone will be able to explain these abilities of hers, at least theoretically, and to figure out whether or not they are inherent in other people as well. Anastasia herself tried to explain how she happens to know about them, only her explanations were difficult to understand.

In any case, I shall try to describe the following situation in its proper order.

CHAPTER TWENTY-ONE

Where do we go in sleep?

On several occasions Anastasia's description of earthly civilisations contained references to the existence of life on other
planets and in other galaxies of the Universe. And I got so
interested in this that while I was listening to her tale about
mankind's past, I could only think about how life evolved out
there, on other planets.

Anastasia, no doubt, saw my interest in her story waning,
and stopped talking. I was quiet, too, thinking about how
I could get her to tell in more specific detail about life in
extraterrestrial civilisations. I could have asked her directly,
of course, but she tends to get somehow distracted whenever
she can't explain why she knows something others don't. And
it seems to me that her desire not to stand out from other
people on account of her abilities discourages her from talking about everything. I've begun noticing, for example, that
she's rather shy about her inability to explain how certain
phenomena work. This is in fact what happened when I
asked her directly:

"Tell me, Anastasia, are you able to teleport yourself
in space? I mean: moving your body from one place to
another?"

"Why are you asking me about that, Vladimir?"

"First tell me specifically: yes or no?"

"Vladimir, everybody has that kind of ability. But I am not
sure I can explain to you just how natural this process is. You
will only withdraw yourself from me again, saying I'm a witch.
You will feel uncomfortable with me."

"So that means you can?"

"I can," she answered hesitantly, her head bowed.

"Then give me a demonstration. Show me how it happens."

"Perhaps I should try to explain first..."

"No, Anastasia, first show me. It's always more interesting to watch something than to listen. And then you can explain."

Anastasia had an estranged look about her as she rose to her feet. She closed her eyes, tensed up a little, and then disappeared before my eyes. Dumbstruck, I looked all around. I even felt with my hands the spot where she had just been standing, but all that was there was some trampled grass, while Anastasia was nowhere to be seen. Then I caught sight of her standing on the far side of the lake. I looked at her, speechless. Then she called out:

"Shall I swim to you? Or shall I once more...?"

"Once more!" I replied and, taking care not to blink in case I missed anything, I began watching the figure of Anastasia standing on the other side of the small lake. All at once she vanished. Simply dissolved into thin air. Not even a trace of smoke was left at the place where I had just seen her. I continued to stand there unblinkingly.

"I am here, Vladimir." Anastasia's voice sounded right beside me. Once again she was standing no more than a metre away. I found myself stepping back a little, then I sat down on the ground, trying not to show any sense of surprise or excitement. For some reason the thought came that suddenly she might take it into her head to dissolve *my* body and then not assemble it afterward.

Anastasia spoke first. "Only the owner of a body can fully dissolve it or split it into atoms. This is an ability available only to Man, Vladimir."

I realised she was going to first try to prove to me that she was Man, and so as not to have her waste any time, I said:

"I realise that it's only given to Man. But surely not to every Man."

"Not to everyone. One must—"

"I know what you're going to say: *One must have pure thoughts.*"

"Yes. Pure thoughts, and besides that, the ability to think quickly and in images, to visualise in specific detail one's self, one's body and desire, a strong will, and faith in one's self..."

"Don't explain, Anastasia. Don't waste your time trying. Tell me rather, can you move your body to any place at all?"

"*Any place,* yes, though I rarely do that. *Any place* can be very dangerous... Besides, there is no need to. Why move one's body? There are other ways..."

"Why dangerous?"

"It is essential to get an accurate picture of the place you wish to move your body to."

"And if you don't get an accurate picture, what can happen?"

"Your body might be lost."

"How?"

"For example, suppose you wanted to transport your body to the floor of the ocean, and the water pressure crushes it. Or you suffocate. Or you might wind up on a city street in front of an oncoming car, and the car hits your body and injures it."

"And can Man also transport his body to another planet?"

"Distance plays absolutely no role here. It will move itself to whatever place your thought dictates. After all, your thought goes to the destination first. It is also what assembles and puts together again the body that was earlier dissolved in space."

"If I wanted to dissolve my body, what should I be thinking about?"

"You have to visualise all of its matter, right down to the tiniest atom, right to the nucleus, and see how the particles create an outwardly chaotic movement in the nucleus, and then mentally dissolve them in space. Then assemble them in their former sequence, in their outwardly chaotic movement in the nucleus, reproducing it accurately. It is all very simple. Just the way children play with blocks."

"But mightn't it turn out that on another planet there wouldn't be a suitable atmosphere to breathe?"

"That is what I am saying — it is dangerous to transport one's body without thinking it through carefully. There are a lot of things to take into account ahead of time."

"So that means it won't work out to go to another planet?"

"It can. It is possible to take some of the surrounding atmosphere along, too, and the body will live in that for a time. But generally it is better not to transport one's body without a particular need for it. In most cases it is sufficient to watch from a distance with one's ray, or transport only one's second, non-material self."

"Incredible! It's hard to believe that every Man was once capable of doing something like that!"

"Why do you say *once*? One's second human self is capable even now of moving about freely, and it does move. Only people do not assign it any specific tasks. They do not set it any goal."

"Who... — what kind of people does this happen with?"

"Right now it basically happens when a person sleeps. It is possible to do the same when one is awake, but on account of the general bustle as well as all sorts of dogmas and various contrived problems, people are losing more and more the ability to control their own selves. They are losing the capacity for imaginative thinking."[1]

---

[1] *imaginative thinking* (Russian: *obraznoe myshlenie*) — the Russian term refers to the specific ability to visualise in one's mind a vivid and detailed image, not just a fantasy.

"Maybe because it's not that interesting to travel without one's body?"

"Why would you think that? In terms of what you feel, the final result can often be the same."

"Well, if the result were the same, people wouldn't go dragging their bodies around, travelling to different countries. Right now the tourist business is pretty profitable in our world. And there's something I don't quite understand about that mysterious second self of Man's. If one's body hasn't been somewhere, that means the Man wasn't there either. It's just as simple and clear as that."

"Do not try to jump to hasty conclusions, Vladimir. I shall now present you with three different scenarios. And you try to tell me in which case this hypothetical person actually took a trip."

"Okay, go ahead."

"Here is the first... Imagine yourself or some other person sound asleep. He is placed on a stretcher. While still asleep, he is put on an aeroplane and taken to another country — from Moscow to Jerusalem, for example. Still sleeping, he is driven up and down the main street, taken into the main temple, and still asleep, brought back the same way and put back where he started. What do you think — was the traveller from Moscow really in Jerusalem?"

"Tell me the other two scenarios first."

"Fine. The second traveller went to Jerusalem all on his own, walked along the main street, spent a little time in the temple and then went home."

"And the third?"

"He left his body behind. But he had the ability to visualise everything at a distance. He walked around the city as though in a dream. He visited the temple, dropped in somewhere else, and then mentally returned to his previous activities... Now, who of the three was actually in Jerusalem, do you think?"

"In the fullest sense, only one of the three was there. That was the one who consciously decided to make the journey and see everything for himself."

"Let us say that is so, but in the final analysis, what did each of them get out of the visit?"

"The first traveller didn't get anything out of it. The second was able to tell about everything he saw. As for the third... The third person would probably also be able to talk about it, only he might make mistakes, since he saw everything in a dream, and a dream can be quite different from reality."

"But the dream as a phenomenon is also a reality."

"Well, yes, the dream exists as a phenomenon. Maybe it's a reality too, but what are you getting at?"

"At the fact, which you will probably not deny, that Man is always able to connect or make contact between two existing realities."

"I know what you've been driving at here. You want to say that it's possible to control a dream and direct it where you want."

"Yes."

"But what exactly helps that come about?"

"It comes about with the help of the energy of thought, and its ability to free any reality for penetration into images."

"And what then, does it register an impression of everything that goes on in some other country, like a TV camera?"

"Excellent! The TV camera can serve as a primitive confirmation. So, Vladimir, you have reached the conclusion that it is not always necessary to transport material bodies to feel what is happening in a faraway land?"

"Perhaps not always. But why did you start telling me about this? Are you trying to prove something?"

"I realised that when you began talking about other worlds that you would demand or ask that I show them to you. I want to carry out your request without putting your body at risk."

"You guessed everything right, Anastasia. I really was going to ask you about that. So, there's life on other planets after all? Gosh, it'd be jolly interesting to see them!"

"Which planet would you like to visit?"

"What — are there a lot of them — inhabited, I mean?"

"There are a great many, though none more interesting than the Earth."

"But still, what kind of life is there on the others? And how did it originate?"

"When the Earth appeared as a Divine co-creation, many of the elements of the Universe were eager to repeat this marvellous creation. They wanted to create their own on other worlds, using planets which in their opinion were suitable. They began creating them, but nobody could create life in a harmony anything like that of the Earth.

"There is in the Universe, for example, a planet where ants predominate over everything. There are a great number of ants on it. The ants devour other life-forms. When there is nothing left for them to eat, they turn to eating each other and die. And the element that created this kind of life is trying to re-create it anew, but it certainly is not turning out any better. Nobody has been able to bring all the elements together in harmony.

"There are also planets where the elements have tried, and are still trying, to create a vegetative world similar to the Earth. And they are creating it. Those planets are growing trees, grass and bushes. But each time their creations reach full maturity they die. None of the elements of the Universe has been able to guess the secret of reproduction. They are like Man today. After all, Man today has created a lot of artificial things all on its own. But not one of his creations can reproduce itself. They break down, rot away, decay and demand constant maintenance. The majority of people on the Earth have been turned into slaves of their own creations. Only the creations of God are capable of reproducing themselves and living in harmony in all their great diversity."

"But are there planets in the Universe, Anastasia, where beings are involved in technology the way Man is?"

"Yes, there are, Vladimir. There is a planet that has six times the Earth's volume and has beings outwardly similar to Man. Their technology is artificial, and has been perfected far beyond the technology of our Earth. Life on this planet was created by an element of the Universe which believes itself to be on a par with God, and is striving for predominance over God's creations."

"Tell me, are they the ones who have come to the Earth in their space ships — the 'flying saucers' we see?"

"Yes. They have tried to make contact with Earth people on a number of occasions. But for the Earth their contacts—"

"No, wait. Is there any way you can take me, or my second self, to that planet for a visit?"

"Yes, I can."

"Then take me there."

After that Anastasia asked me to lie down on the ground and relax. Telling me to spread out my arms to the sides, she placed one of her hands in mine and in a short time I began to doze off into something similar to sleep. I say *something similar,* as this dozing off was most unusual. First my body felt more and more relaxed. I couldn't feel my body any more, though I could see and hear everything around me perfectly well — the singing of the birds, the rustling of the leaves. Then I closed my eyes and sank into a sleep, or 'divided myself' (as Anastasia would put it). But to this day I am not in a position to say what happened to me next or how. If it is to be assumed that with Anastasia's help I fell asleep and had a dream, the fulness of my sensations and the clarity of my awareness of everything I saw can in no way be compared with any human dream.

CHAPTER TWENTY TWO

Other worlds

I saw another world, another planet. I was able to remember everything that went on there in clear detail, yet to this day I still have the lingering feeling in my consciousness that beholding anything like that is an impossibility. Think about it — my mind and consciousness tell me it's impossible, and yet they — the visions, the pictures — remain with me to this day. And now I shall try and describe them to you.

I stood on ground similar to what we have on the Earth. There was absolutely no vegetation around me. I say *stood*. But whether I can actually say that it's hard to tell. I didn't have any legs or arms, I didn't even have a body, and yet at the same time it seemed I could feel my steps, I could feel the rocky, uneven surface through the soles of my feet.

All around, as far as the eye could see, above the soil rose metallic machines, both egg-shaped ones and square, or cube-like machines. I use the word *machines* because the one closest to me gave off a kind of soft whirring sound.

From each of these machines a plethora of hoses of different diameters went down into the ground. Some of these hoses were slightly quivering, as though something was being sucked up through them from the ground, while others were in a motionless state. No living beings were in sight.

All at once I saw a panel on the side of one of these strange devices open, and out floated — rather slowly — a kind of disc, similar in shape to a discus thrown by athletes, only much larger, about forty-five metres in diameter. It hovered in the air, and then started to rotate. After a brief descent it took off and flew completely noiselessly overhead. Other devices a little further away did the same, and several more discs flew after the first one, one after the other, right over my head. And then once again there was just still and empty space, except for the whirring and crackling of the strange devices. The whole picture aroused my interest, but even more, its indescribable lifelessness was frightening.

"Do not be afraid of anything, Vladimir." All at once I caught the sound of Anastasia's voice, which comforted me no end.

"Where are you, Anastasia?" I enquired.

"Right here beside you. We are invisible, Vladimir. Present here are our feelings, sensations, mind and all our other invisible forms of energy. We are here without our material bodies. Nobody can do anything to us. The only thing we need be wary of is ourselves, and the consequences of our own sensations."

"What kind of consequences might there be?"

"Psychological consequences. Like temporarily going out of one's mind."

"Going out of one's mind?"

"Yes, but only temporarily. For a month or two, it can happen: the vision of other planets may stir up Man's mind and consciousness. But you need not be afraid, you are not threatened by this. You will pull through. And there is nothing to be afraid of — believe me, Vladimir, you are indeed here, but not as far as they are concerned. At the moment we are invisible and can go and see whatever we wish to."

"I'm not afraid. Only you'd better tell me, Anastasia, what are those whirring machines all around us? What are they for?"

"Each of those egg-shaped machines is a factory. They are the ones that produce the 'flying saucers' that are of such interest to you."

"And who maintains, or controls these factories?"

"No one. They are programmed in advance to make a particular product. Through those pipes going down into the ground they suck up the raw material they need in the required amounts. The forging and pressing, and then the assembly, all take place in small compartments inside, and then the fully formed product comes out. This factory is much more efficient than any on the Earth. There is practically no waste from this process. There is no need to transport raw material from distant places. There is no need to ship individual component parts to the assembly point. The whole manufacturing process is concentrated in one place."

"Amazing! We should have a gizmo like that! And who controls the new 'flying saucers'? I noticed they were all flying in the same direction."

"Nobody controls them, they fly all by themselves to a storage depot."

"Incredible! Just like a living being!"

"But this by itself represents nothing incredible, even in terms of earthly technology. After all, the Earth also has pilotless planes and rockets."

"Just the same, they are controlled by people on the Earth."

"But the Earth for a long time has also had rockets which are preprogrammed for a specific target. All one has to do is push the launch button and the rocket fires itself and heads for a predetermined target."

"Maybe so. And really, what was there here that was so surprising?"

"If you really think about it, there is not that much to be surprised at. Only, by comparison with the technology we have on the Earth, this is far more advanced. These factories, Vladimir, are multifunctional. They can manufacture a great deal, from food products to powerful weapons."

"And what are their food products made of? Nothing grows here, after all."

"Everything comes from deep in the ground. The machines take in all the juices they need through the pipes and press them into granules. These granules will contain all the substances needed to sustain bodily life."

"What does this gizmo itself feed on? Who supplies it with electrical power? I don't see any wires."

"It produces the energy it needs all on its own, using everything from the environment."

"Well, just look how smart it is! Smarter than Man."

"It is by no means smarter than Man, Vladimir. It is simply a machine. It is subject to its assigned programme, and is very easy to reprogram. Would you like me to show you how it is done?"

"Go ahead."

"Let us move a little closer to it."

We stood at about a metre's distance from the huge device, which was the size of a nine-storey building. The crackling sound became more distinct. An army of flexible tentacle-like pipes reached into the ground, shaking. The surface of the device's covering wasn't entirely smooth. I caught sight of a circular area approximately a metre in diameter, densely covered with small wires sticking out like hairs. They were quivering, each one individually.

"This is the antenna for the scanning apparatus. It picks up the brain's energy impulses which it uses to compile a programme capable of carrying out an assigned task. If your brain can visualise a particular object, the machine should be able to manufacture it."

"Any object?"

"Any that you can picture in detail. As though constructing it with your thoughts."

"And any kind of car?"

"Of course."

"And can I try it right now?"

"Yes. Move closer to the receiver and start by mentally instructing its antenna to turn all its receptor wires toward you. Directly that happens, begin picturing what you desire."

I stood close to the wiry antenna. Burning with curiosity, I mentally desired, as Anastasia had said, to have all its wires pay heed to me. At first they turned in my direction, then all of them, with a slight trembling, directed their tips to my invisible head and stayed still.

Now I had to visualise a particular object. For some reason I began picturing a Model 7 Zhiguli[1] — the car I had in Novosibirsk. I tried picturing everything in as much detail as I could — the window-glass and the bonnet, the bumper, the colour and even the licence plate. I took a long time with the visualisation. When I got tired of it, I moved away from the antenna. The huge machine started whirring more briskly."

"We must wait," explained Anastasia. "Now it is disassembling the unfinished product it was working on and compiling a programme for carrying out your design."

"Will we have long to wait?"

"I do not think so."

We went over to look at some of the other machines. Presently, as I was examining the multicoloured rocks underfoot, I heard Anastasia's voice announcing:

"I think the manufacture of the object you pictured in your mind is complete. Let us take a look and see how it coped with the task."

[1]*Zhiguli* — a car first produced in the late 1960s at the Volga Automobile Factory at Toliatti, on the Volga River, by an agreement with the Italian Fiat corporation. The cars outwardly resemble a Fiat of about the same era, and are still being produced to this date.

We went back to the first machine and began waiting. After a little while its panel opened and out came a Zhiguli. It rolled down a smooth ramp to the ground. But this freak standing in front of me had nothing on the beautiful automobile I knew back on the Earth.

First, it had only one door — one on the driver's side. In place of the back seats there were only some coils of wire and pieces of rubber. I walked — or rather moved — around the object. It was definitely not something you could call a motor car.

Two wheels were missing from the passenger side. Nor was there any bumper or licence plate at the front. The bonnet did not look as though it would open — it seemed to be made of a single piece with the chassis. In sum, this unique factory had produced not a car, but some kind of narwhal of indeterminate function.

And I said:

"Gawd! Is that the best this alien factory can come up with? If this had happened on Earth, they'd have sacked all the designers and engineers!"

Anastasia burst out laughing in response, and I heard her voice say:

"Of course they might have been let go. But in this case the chief designer is you, Vladimir, and what you see is the product of your designing."

"I wanted a standard modern automobile, but what has this machine spit out?"

"Wanting is not enough. You have to picture everything down to the minutest detail. You did not even include any passenger doors in your visualisation. You only thought of the one door for yourself. And you pictured wheels only on your side of the car — you neglected to put in wheels on the other side. And I think you completely forgot about the motor."

"Completely forgot."

"Which means there is no motor in your design. So why blame the manufacturer when you yourself gave it an incomplete programme to work with?"

All at once I saw, or sensed, the approach of three flying machines heading in our direction. *Gotta get outa here* — the thought flashed across my mind, but then I heard Anastasia's calming voice:

"They will not notice us or sense us in any way, Vladimir. They have received word about a disruption in the work of one of their factories, and now they are probably coming to investigate. We shall have the opportunity to quietly observe some of the living inhabitants of this planet."

Out of the three small flying machines stepped five aliens. They were very similar in appearance to earthlings. Not just similar, but everything about them suggested earthlings. They were well built. No slouching shoulders — their athletic bodies held their handsome heads straight and proud. And they even had hair on their heads and eyebrows on their faces, and one of them sported a neatly trimmed moustache. They were dressed in thin multicoloured one-piece outfits that tightly covered their whole body.

The aliens walked over to the car produced by their factory, or, more accurately, to the semblance of an earthly car. They stood silently beside it, observing, without emotion. *They are no doubt having one hell of a time trying to figure this one out,* I thought.

The alien who appeared to be the youngest, with light-brown hair, detached himself from the others. He went up to the door of the car and tried to open it, but the door refused to budge. The lock was probably jammed. The rest of his actions seemed very earthly, which gave me no small comfort. The brown-haired alien banged his hand on the door in the area of the lock, then tried pulling it harder this time, and the door opened. He sat down in the driver's seat, put his hands on the steering-wheel and began to carefully examine the dashboard instruments.

Good lad, I thought. *A clever fellow.* And in confirmation of my appraisal I heard Anastasia say:

"This is a very top-ranked scientist, by their standards, Vladimir. His thought works quickly and logically in a technical orientation. Besides, he is studying how beings live on several other planets, including the Earth. He even has an Earth-like name — Arkaan."

"But why does his face show no surprise at finding that one of their factories made something anomalous?"

"The inhabitants of this planet have almost no feelings or emotions. Their minds work evenly and logically, with no giving in to emotional outbursts or departures from set goals."

The young alien climbed out of the car, uttering sounds reminiscent of Morse code. An older alien stepped forward and stood by the wiry antenna where I had positioned myself earlier. Then they all climbed back into their flying machines and took off.

The factory which had manufactured the car according to my design began whirring again. Its tentacle pipes began pulling themselves up from the ground and redirecting themselves toward a nearby automated factory of the same type, from which tentacle pipes also extended. When all the tentacles joined together, Anastasia said:

"You see, they have reprogrammed it to self-destruct. All the components of the factory where the disruption occurred will now be remoulded by the other factory and used in production."

And I began feeling a trifle sorry for the robot factory which had helped me create, albeit unsuccessfully, an Earth-car. But there was absolutely nothing I could do about it.

"Vladimir, would you like to take a look at the everyday life of the planet's inhabitants?" Anastasia offered.

"Yes, of course."

We found ourselves overlooking one of the cities or settlements of the huge planet. Our aerial view afforded us the following picture:

As far as the eye could see, the whole populated area consisted of a great many cylindrical installations, something like our modern skyscrapers, set in a large number of circles. In the centre of each circle were low-rise structures somewhat reminiscent of trees on the Earth — even their sensor-leaves were green. And Anastasia confirmed that these artificial structures draw up from the ground all the components of substances needed for sustenance, which are then despatched through special pipes into the homes of every inhabitant of this particular world. Not only that but they maintain the requisite atmosphere for the planet.

When Anastasia suggested paying a visit to one of the apartments, I asked:

"Can we visit the flat of that brown-haired alien who sat in my car?"

"Yes," she replied. "At this moment he will be just getting home from work."

We found ourselves almost at the very top of one of the cylindrical skyscrapers. There were absolutely no windows in this alien apartment block. The circular walls were marked off into dull-coloured squares. Near the bottom of each square was a raisable door — the kind you might find on our modern garages. Now and then one of the doors would open and out would come a small flying machine similar to the ones we had seen near the automated factory, and fly off on its own. It turned out that there was a small garage for one of these machines located below each apartment in the high-rise.

There were no lifts or doors in the building. Each flat had its own entrance directly from the garage. And, as it turned out, every inhabitant of the planet acquired an apartment like this once he reached a certain age.

At first I didn't particularly take to the flat itself. Upon finding ourselves in the brown-haired man's flat just after he arrived home, my initial impression was one of surprise at its simplicity and apparent lack of amenities. The room, approximately thirty square metres in area, was completely barren. It wasn't just that there were no windows or partitions — there wasn't even the barest modicum of furniture. The smooth, pale walls bore not a single painting or shelf by way of decoration.

"Maybe he's just got this flat recently?" I asked Anastasia.

"Arkaan has been living here for twenty years now. His apartment has everything necessary for relaxation, entertainment and work. All the necessary components are built into the walls. You shall presently see for yourself."

Indeed, no sooner had the brown-haired alien come up from his garage below, than the ceiling and walls of the room began to glow with a soft light. Arkaan turned to face the wall next to the entrance, placed the palm of his hand on the surface and uttered a sound. A panel on the wall lit up.

Anastasia gave a running commentary on everything that was taking place in the apartment:

"Right now the computer is identifying the apartment's owner by the lines of his hand and his eye-scan. Now it is greeting him and letting him know how long he has been gone, as well as the need to check his physical condition... You see, Vladimir, Arkaan has put his other hand up to the console and is letting out a deep sigh so that the computer can check his physical condition... Now the check-up is complete, and a message has appeared on the screen telling him he needs to take a nutrient mixture. It is asking him what he intends to do over the next three hours.

"This is important for the computer to know in order to prepare an appropriate mixture. Now Arkaan is asking for a mixture optimised to boost his mental activity for the next three hours, after which he intends to go to sleep.

"The computer is suggesting that he not engage in any strenuous mental activity over a three hour period; instead, it is recommending he take a solution calculated to sustain work activity for a period of two hours and sixteen minutes. Arkaan has agreed to the computer's recommendation."

At that point a small niche opened in the wall, from which Arkaan seized hold of a flexible pipe. Putting the end of the hose to his mouth he took a drink (or a bite to eat) from the hose and then went over to the opposite wall. The niche holding the pipe closed up, the screen panel dimmed, and the wall where the alien had just been standing once more became smooth and monochrome.

Wow! I thought, with this technology you can do away with a kitchen and all its equipment, and dishes, and furniture — especially you can do away with clean-up. And even with a wife who knows how to make a good meal. No need to go to the store. Besides, at one fell swoop the computer can check your health, prepare the food you require and make all sorts of recommendations. I wonder how much a computer would cost back on the Earth? And immediately I heard Anastasia say:

"As for expenditures, it is less expensive to equip each apartment with such a device than to load kitchens down with furniture and a whole lot of appliances for food preparation. They are much more rational than earthlings, all told. But in fact there is much more rationality on the Earth than here."

I didn't pay much attention to Anastasia's last remark. I was too absorbed in watching Arkaan's actions. He went on giving voice commands, and the following events ensued in the room.

From a section of the wall all at once an armchair began to inflate. Then beside the chair another little niche opened, from which a small table emerged, along with some kind of semi-transparent container resembling a laboratory flask. On the opposite wall of the room a large screen lit up, about one-and-a-half to two metres in diagonal. The screen showed a beautiful woman in a slinky body-suit seated in a comfortable chair. The woman was holding a container in her hands similar to the one on the table beside Arkaan. The image of the woman on the screen was three-dimensional, and much sharper than on our TV sets. It seemed as though she were not on a screen, but sitting right there in the room.

Anastasia explained that Arkaan and the woman sitting opposite him were forming a child together.

"The inhabitants of this planet do not have sufficient strength of feeling to enter into sexual relations like people on the Earth. Outwardly their bodies are no different. But the absence of feelings does not allow them to produce offspring the way people do on the Earth. It is their own cells and hormones that are contained in the test-tubes you see. Men and women visualise what they would like their future child to look like. They mentally instil in him the information they themselves contain, and discuss his future activity. This process lasts approximately three years in Earth time. Once they determine that the process of the child's formation is complete, they join the contents of the two containers together in a special laboratory, the child is produced and raised in a special nursery school until he comes of age. Then as a mature member of the community he is offered an apartment and assigned to the personnel roster of one of the work groups."

Arkaan alternated his gaze between the woman on the screen and the liquid in the little sealed container. All at once the wall screen dimmed, but the alien remained seated in his chair, his eyes fixed on the container on the table in front of him holding a particle of his future child. Now the opposite wall was flashing with red squares. The alien turned sideways, his hands shielding his eyes from the flashing lights, and inclined his head even closer to his container. New illuminated squares and triangles began flashing alarmingly from the ceiling.

"The wake-time allotted Arkaan by the computer has expired. Now the computer is insistently reminding him of the need for sleep," Anastasia explained.

But the alien bent his head down even closer to his flask, clasping it in his hands.

The lights on the walls and the ceiling stopped flashing. The room began filling with some kind of steam-like gas. Anastasia's voice remarked:

"Now the computer is using gas to put Arkaan to sleep."

The alien's head began slowly drooping toward the table and soon it was resting on it, his eyes closed. The armchair began emerging even further out of the wall and transforming itself into a bed. Then the bed-chair began rocking from side to side, and the body of the already sleeping alien fell back into a comfortable cradle.

Arkaan slept clasping the little container in his hands to his chest.

There is so much more to tell about the advanced technological features not only of the apartment, but on the huge planet as a whole. According to Anastasia, the community of people inhabiting it have no fear of any invasion from the outside. Not only that, but with the help of their technical achievements they are capable of destroying life on any other planet in the Universe. Any except the Earth.

"Why?" I asked. "Does that mean our rockets and weapons are capable of repelling an attack?" And Anastasia replied:

"Earth rockets pose no threat to them, Vladimir. The civilisation on this planet has long been acquainted with all the derivatives of explosion. They also are familiar with implosion."

"What does that mean, *implosion?*"

"Scientists on the Earth know that when two or more substances which have come together in an instantaneous reaction expand, an explosion occurs. But there is a different reaction from contact between two substances. Take a gaseous substance, about a cubic kilometre or more in size, capable of instantaneously compressing itself to the size of a speck, thereby becoming a super-hard material. Imagine a grenade or a rocket exploding in such a cloud, but another force simultaneously acting against the explosion — an implosion — will take place at the same time. And all you will hear then is a clapping sound. And everything that was in that cloud will be transformed into a stone the size of a speck. All the rockets on Earth will not overcome the pall of gaseous clouds.

"In the history of the Earth there have been two comings, or invasions, on their part. Now they are preparing for a third. They think a favourable moment for that is once more approaching."

"That means nothing can stop them, if there are no weapons on Earth stronger than theirs."

"Man does have a weapon. It is known as *Man's thought.* Even I alone could turn about half of their weapons into dust and scatter them through the Universe. And if I could find some helpers, then together we would be able to liquidate all their weapons. The only thing is, the majority of people on the Earth and almost all the governments on the Earth would consider their invasion a blessing."

"But how could it happen that everyone took an invasion, an attack, for a blessing?"

"You will see in a moment. Here, take a look at the centre which is preparing an invasion force to take over the continents of the Earth."

CHAPTER TWENTY-THREE

The invasion centre

Of course I was eager to see their interplanetary super-technology that was capable of conquering a whole planet. But what my eyes actually saw... I think our Russian, American and other military strategists have absolutely no idea of the kind of weapons that could so easily be used to take over the territories they are supposedly protecting.

And you, dear readers, before you read on, try to imagine how an alien centre preparing for an invasion of the Earth might be equipped. And then look and see what it looks like in reality. I shall now attempt to describe its outward appearance.

A huge square room. Along each of the four walls there is a life-size replica of the interiors of our own native parliaments on the Earth. Along one wall is the State Duma,[1] along with the office of our President in the Kremlin. On the opposite wall I could see the interiors of the American Congress and the office of the American president in the White House. Along the other two walls were the offices of various State political institutions — in some of the Asian countries, judging by their appearance.

In the parliamentary seats were sitting our earthling deputies,[2] congressmen and presidents. First of all I began examining our own Russian deputies. They were an exact copy of

[1]*Duma* — the Russian Parliament (derived from the Russian word meaning 'to think').

[2]*deputies* — members of the *Duma* are known as *deputaty* (deputies).

the familiar faces I had seen on TV. Only here they were sitting motionless, like mummies. It is difficult to say what they were made of. Maybe they were dolls, holograms or robots, or maybe even something else.

In the middle of the huge hall was a raised platform, on which were sitting approximately fifty aliens. They were dressed not in their usual bodysuits, but in our earthly clothing, and were listening to a speaker standing in front of them. Probably their chief instructor or some other official.

Anastasia explained that we were observing one of the landing parties, currently engaged in a routine class session on preparing for interaction with earthly governments. They have been studying the most common Earth languages and the way people behave in various situations. They are paying special attention to the preparation for contact with governments and legislative bodies, through which they hope to influence the whole population of the Earth.

They have mastered conversational speech without too much difficulty, but in the absence of certain feelings capable of provoking outward emotions, they are finding it rather hard to mimic Earth people's gestures. And with their rationalistic way of thinking they cannot see any logic in earthly governmental systems. Despite their drawing upon the best minds and the most modern technology of their civilisation, they have still been unable to guess, for example, the secret of why, in spite of the computer technology already available on the Earth and the multitude of special scientific institutions, our national legislative bodies are still not provided with information about the consequences of the decisions they take. They are convinced that were there a specific analysis centre — a 'think tank', in other words — for which everything requisite is already available on the Earth, it would be possible to visualise almost perfectly the social consequences of all parliamentary decisions. Instead, every legislator, every member of an earthly government, is obliged to make decisions independently. Not having sufficient information at their fingertips, each member of a government is obliged to fulfil the function of a powerful analysis centre and calculate the consequences not only of his own actions but also those of his colleagues, enemies and friends.

Another very mysterious question which the aliens have not been able to guess the answer to is why earthlings do not define any goal to be attained. They aspire to something, but to what — that remains a deep secret. Nevertheless, on the basis of the current requirements of earthly societies the aliens have prepared a plan to invade Earth's continents. They will begin by making proposals to earthlings through the governments of various countries. And their proposals will be accepted with great enthusiasm.

When I asked Anastasia why she was so confident in governmental acceptance of the proposals, she replied as follows:

"This is what their analysis centre has determined. The conclusions of the centre are correct. Given the level of conscious awareness of most earthlings today, they will take the aliens' proposal as a supreme manifestation of the humanity of the Mind of the Universe."

"And what kind of proposals are they?"

"They are monstrous, Vladimir. It is difficult for me even to talk about them."

"Tell me at least the main points. It would be interesting, after all, to know just what these monstrous proposals are that would be enthusiastically welcomed on the Earth — the Earth I live on, and you too."

"The aliens first plan to land a small party, three of their flying machines, on Russian territory. They will tell the military personnel which surround them of their desire to meet with government circles to talk about mutual co-operation. They will present themselves to the soldiers as representatives of

the Supreme Mind of the Universe and give them a demonstration of their superior technology.

"After military, scientific and government circles have held
internal consultations, approximately fourteen days later the
aliens will be invited to concretise their proposals, but first
they will have to undergo a medical examination to make sure
it is safe to communicate with them.

"The aliens will agree to the medical examination and then
put their proposals in writing, as well as on video. The text
will be laid out in a form very similar to our modern official
documents, and will be characterised by extreme simplicity.

"The text will read something like this:

*We the representatives of an extraterrestrial civilisation, hav-
ing achieved the ultimate level of technological development by
comparison with other intelligent inhabitants of the Universe, do
hereby consider Earth people our brothers in reason.*

*We are prepared to share our knowledge with societies on the
Earth in various branches of science and social structure and offer them our technology.*

*We ask you to consider our proposals and select the ones most
suitable for improving the life of every member of your society.*

"Then will follow a whole series of concrete proposals, the
substance of which amounts to this:

"The visitors offer to share their technology in providing
each citizen of the country with nutrient mixture and rapid
construction of housing for everyone who has reached the age
of maturity. This is the same kind of housing you have already
seen, Vladimir, only with not quite so many functions. As an
example, they will introduce their mini-factories into the
country. They will integrate their alien factories with existing
Earth factories, but in five years all Earth technologies will
be discarded and replaced by technologically more advanced

counterparts. A job will be guaranteed for all who wish to have one. Not only that, but every single inhabitant of the Earth will be required to contribute a certain minimum amount of work toward maintaining the technological devices.

"A nation that signs a treaty with the visitors will be completely protected from military invasion by any other nation. In a society which embraces the new social order and its technologically supported lifestyle there will be no crime. In the apartments provided you, everything you need will react only to your voice commands, identified by tones inherent only in your voice. Every day before you take in food, the computers in your apartments will scan your eyes, breath and other parameters to determine your physical health and prescribe the corresponding food mixture composition.

"Each computer installed in an individual apartment will be linked with the main computer, which will thereby be able to pinpoint the exact geographic location of every individual, along with his state of physical and mental health. Any criminal offence will be easily uncovered with the help of a special programme in the main computer. Besides, the social conditions which now foster crime will be absent.

"In return, the visitors plan to ask the government's permission to settle representatives of their civilisation in sparsely inhabited areas — mainly in forests — as well as the right of people to exchange their individual garden plots for technologically equipped apartments and provision of lifetime care if they choose to do so.

"The governments will agree, under the impression that they will still be in full control. A number of religious denominations will start preaching that the alien visitors are God's emissaries, since the aliens will not deny any of the religions existing on the Earth. Religious leaders who do not believe in the aliens' Divine perfection will find it impossible to stand up against the visitors since they will be accepted by the majority of the citizens in each country that signs the treaty. All other countries will start seeking similar treaties of co-operation with the visitors.

"Nine years after the first landing on the Earth a new way of life will have been speedily inculcated into all countries on all the continents of the Earth. All information media will broadcast the ever advancing achievements in technology and social order. The majority of the population will glorify the 'emissaries of the Mind of the Universe' as intellectually superior brethren, as deities in themselves."

"And not without justification," I remarked to Anastasia. "There's nothing wrong in having no wars and crime on the Earth. Everyone will be provided with an apartment, food and employment."

"Vladimir, do you not realise that once mankind accepts the terms of the aliens, they at the same time renounce their non-material, Divine self? In fact, it will self-destruct. All that is left will be material bodies. And every Man, Vladimir, will come to more and more resemble a biological robot. And all the children of the Earth will henceforth be born biological robots."

"But why?"

"All people on the Earth will be compelled to render daily service to those devices which outwardly serve them. All mankind will fall into a trap, surrendering their own freedom and that of their children for the sake of an artificial technological perfection. Before long many Earth people will intuitively recognise their mistake and start ending their lives by suicide."

"Strange. What would they be lacking?"

"Freedom, creativity and the feelings that only co-creation with the Divine creation can bring."

"And if the parliaments and governments of various countries are unwilling to sign treaties with the aliens, what then? Will they start destroying mankind?"

"Then the alien minds will look for other ways to lead everybody into a trap. There is no sense in their annihilating mankind. After all, their goal is to understand the inter-relationship among all earthly creations, and by what power reproduction is brought about. Nothing like that can exist without Man. It is Man who is the chief link in the chain of harmony of earthly creation. And the Sun's rays are part of the energy and feelings that many people reproduce. With their present level of consciousness today's Earth people pose no resistance to the visitors. And many earthlings today are even trying to render them assistance."

"How so? Who among us is trying to help them? Does that mean there are traitors in our midst? Working for them?"

"They are working for them, but these people are not traitors. Their acquiescence in this comes about involuntarily — it is without malice or premeditation. The main reason is their own lack of faith in themselves and in the perfection of God's creations."

"What's the connection here?"

"It is simple. When Man admits the thought that he is not a perfect creation, when he all at once begins to imagine that there are beings on other planets of superior intellect, he himself feeds them by his own thought. Man himself thereby belittles his own God-given power and attributes power to creations other than the Divine. They have already learnt to gather the energy human thoughts and feelings can produce into a unified complex and are proud of that achievement.

"Look, and you will see in front of that group of aliens there is a container of glowing liquid, which is being transformed back and forth between gaseous, liquid and solid states. They have no weapon stronger than what is concentrated in that small container. Later they will distribute its whole content into a whole lot of small, shallow containers. One of the sides of the container will act as a special reflector. Each one of them will wear a similar device around his neck in the form of a medallion. All the aliens you see sitting in front of you are wearing such devices right now. When a ray from this medallion is directed at a Man, it may provoke in him feelings of fear, reverence or excitement. And it can paralyse not only a person's will, but also his consciousness and his body. This ray contains thoughts of a multitude of people. People's thoughts that there is someone in the Universe stronger than Man. *Stronger than Man, God's creation.* And these thoughts, when concentrated, can be turned against people themselves."

"So, it turns out we ourselves give them power when we consider them mentally superior to ourselves?"

"Yes, that is right. Mentally superior to ourselves means mentally superior to God."

"What's God got to do with it?"

"We are His creations. When we believe that there are other more perfect worlds in the Universe, that means we are accepting ourselves as imperfect — imperfect creations of God."

"Wow! And have they already accumulated a lot of such energy on the alien world?"

"In the container standing in front of you there is enough energy to overcome approximately three quarters of all the minds on the Earth and to take over people's feelings. *That* they consider way more than enough. Then the whole earthly civilisation will begin to pay them obeisance. And their power will increase."

"So, is it impossible at this stage to do anything about it?"

"It is possible, if we take a risk and do something they are not expecting. After all, a full complex of human feelings, even just one, is always stronger. And it is possible to accelerate thought to a speed unknown to those who have no feelings. And all the energy amassed in that container can be neutralised by the energy of another thought which is brighter, more confident and more perfect."

"And you, Anastasia, would you yourself be able to neutralise all the energy in that container?"

"I could try, but I would have to bring my whole body here for that."

"Why?"

"My complex of feelings will not be complete without my body. Matter is one of the planes of Man's being. With it Man is stronger than the elements of the Universe."

"So, go ahead — we need to break the container."

And all at once in front of me I saw Anastasia in the flesh. She was dressed just as she had been in the forest, in a cardigan and skirt. She stood there barefoot on the floor, and then all at once started walking unhurriedly over to the aliens sitting in front of the container with the glowing liquid. They caught sight of her. No emotions showed themselves on the faces of these unfeeling beings — only for a brief moment they remained motionless in their seats. A second later everyone was astir. Suddenly, as if on command, they all rose and grasped hold of the medallions around their necks. All the medallions flashed with rays of light, all directed at the approaching figure of Anastasia.

She stopped, lost her balance momentarily, took a small step backward, then stopped again. Giving a little stamp with her bare foot, she slowly and confidently moved forward again.

The rays coming from the aliens' medallions got brighter and brighter as they joined together, concentrating on Anastasia. It looked as though it would take but a moment for them to reduce all the clothing on her to ashes. But Anastasia continued moving forward. All at once she stretched her hands out in front of her. Some of the rays reflected off the palms of her hands and were extinguished. Then the others started to go out.

The aliens stood there stock still, as before. Anastasia went over to the container, put her hands around it, stroked it with her palms and whispered something to it. All at once the liquid in the container became turbulent, then its glow began to gradually fade, and before long there remained a practically colourless liquid with only a slight bluish tinge, much like ordinary water on the Earth.

Anastasia went over to a machine standing by the wall that looked something like a refrigerator. She pressed her hand against it, whispered something to it, and out came a shower of some kind of small coloured square tablets, which she caught in the upturned hem of her cardigan.

Anastasia went over to the aliens, who were still standing dumbstruck as before, and held out one of the tablets to the one at the end. He stirred, as though about to hold out his hand, but stopped at once and began staring in the direction of the man who was standing in front of them all — probably their leader. And so there was Anastasia standing before him for about half a minute, her hand outstretched.

Then she went over and stood directly in front of the leader and held out a tablet for *him*. After a brief pause the leader took the tablet and put it in his mouth. Anastasia then went around to each one in turn, and this time everyone calmly took a tablet from her and ate or swallowed it.

Then she turned from them and came over toward me. She had got half way to me when all at once she stopped and, turning toward the group of seated aliens, waved her hand at them. And several of the aliens got up from their seats and waved their hand back at her in response. When she reached my position, she said with a tired voice:

"We need to go back. They have now taken the thought-accelerating tablets. Let them try to make sense of what has happened here."

And then it was all over. I found myself lying on the grass as before, as though awakening from sleep. It seemed just a short time had passed, but my body felt rested, as after a deep, healthy sleep. But my head... Inside me everything felt as though it were boiling over. As though my thoughts were running in all directions at once. All the images I had seen on that other planet completely stayed with me.

What was it? A dream? Hypnosis? Or everything at once — it still wasn't clear. To see what is actually happening on a planet other than the Earth — this was something I found impossible to believe, and I asked Anastasia who was sitting beside me:

"What was it? A dream? Hypnosis? I seem to have remembered everything and now my head feels absolutely chaotic."

And she replied:

"Vladimir, as for the power by which this vision of another planet appeared to you, take it any way you like. If you find the question disturbing, you can simply tell yourself you had a dream. Besides, all that is not what is really important. What *is* important is the essence, the conclusions and the sensations of this vision you saw. Think about that while I leave you for a while."

"Yes, go on. I'll be thinking about it here on my own."

Left alone, I began to ponder what I had seen. Naturally I concluded that I had had some kind of hypnotic dream.

After taking just a few steps, however, Anastasia suddenly turned and headed back in my direction. She took something out of the pocket of her cardigan, and held out her open hand to me. And there I saw it, lying on her hand... a strange-looking tablet, the same kind I had seen on the other planet.

"Take it, Vladimir. You need not be afraid to swallow it. On the planet you and I visited they make these out of herbs from here on the Earth. For about fifteen minutes it will help accelerate your thought, and you will be able to make sense of everything all the more quickly."

I took the little tablet from her outstretched hand, and when Anastasia left, I ate it.

CHAPTER TWENTY-FOUR

Take back your Motherland, people!

At first I found my dialogue with Anastasia about what constitutes the *Motherland*[1] rather unintelligible. Her arguments didn't even seem normal to me, at least initially. But later...

Even today I can't help thinking of them. I distinctly recall her response to my questions about what to do to prevent war — either earthly or interplanetary — from happening to us, to eliminate bandits altogether and bear happy and healthy children. It went this way:

"We need to tell everyone, Vladimir: *Take back your Motherland, people!*"

"'Take back your Motherland?' — are you sure you're not mistaken, Anastasia? Everyone has a Motherland, or a native

---

[1]*Motherland* — The Russian term here is *rodina*, also translatable as *native land*. *Rodina* conveys a deep reverence to one's ancestors, responsibility for descendants and an intimate connection to the land one's family lives on. As explained in footnote 2 in Book 2, Chapter 27: "The anomaly", the term *Rodina* is derived from two Russian roots connected by *i* (= 'and'): (a) *Rod* — the name of God the Creator in the ancient Slavic tradition, also signifying 'origin', 'derivation', 'birth', 'kin' and, by extension, 'Father', and (b) *Na* — a root signifying 'Mother', and quite possibly the same root as the *na* in the Latin participle *natus* ('born'), from which our English words *native* and *nature* are derived. Subsequently *Rod i Na* ('Father and Mother') took on the broader significance of one's family (or 'kin'), and by association came to refer to the particular geographical location occupied by succeeding generations of the same family. Readers should be aware that it is the 'native' or 'family' aspect, more than the 'land' component, that is significant in understanding the term *Motherland* (i.e., *Rodina*) in this and subsequent chapters.

land, only not everybody lives in the country where they were born. Maybe you didn't mean '*take back* your Motherland', but 'you need to *come back to* your Motherland' — is that what you were trying to say?"

"I was not mistaken, Vladimir. Most people living on this planet today have no Motherland at all."

"What d'you mean they haven't a Motherland? For Russians, Russia is their Motherland, the English have England. After all, everybody was born somewhere, and so people will use the term *Motherland* or *native land* to refer to the land where they were born."

"Do you consider that one's Motherland must be measured by someone's arbitrarily determined border?"

"What else? That's the way things are. All states have borders."

"But if there were no borders, how could you determine your Motherland then?"

"By the place I was born — the town or village — or maybe the whole Earth would then be a Motherland for everyone?"

"The whole Earth *could* be a Motherland for each one of its inhabitants, and Man could be caressed by everything in the Universe, but for that to happen, he would need to join together all planes of being into a single point, call it his *Motherland,* and create with his own self a Space of Love therein. Then all the best things of the Universe would come into contact with it first hand — come into contact with the space of your Motherland. You in yourself will feel the whole vast Universe through this point, and possess power unsurpassed. They will know about this on other worlds. Everything will serve you, as God, our Creator, wanted it."

"You've really got to speak in simpler terms, Anastasia. I didn't get anything about those 'planes of being', or how to join together their strands. Or about the 'point' I can call my Motherland."

"Then we need to begin our discussion with what constitutes birth."

"Well, okay, with birth then. Only don't just say words, but use words that make sense for us on the Earth today. Tell me, for example, how you see, how you picture the generation of the family — the birth and raising of children — in today's prevailing conditions. And how all the children of Man can be born happy. Can you construct a plan or draw me a picture?"

"I can."

"Then tell me about it. Only not about life in the forest or about the incomprehensible *science of imagery*. Nobody knows anything about that, only you..."

I couldn't finish the sentence. My head was buzzing with not just one but a whole lot of questions. Especially: Why was I even interested in knowing what this taiga recluse would tell me about our lives? How does she happen to know not only the outward details of our lives but many people's inner feelings too? What were the possibilities of this incomprehensible science of imagery?

I couldn't stay seated. I got up and began to pace to and fro. Trying to calm down and to make sense of — to understand — these incredible phenomena, I began to reason like this:

Here's this young woman calmly sitting under a cedar tree — ruffling her hand slowly through the grass, or watching some bug crawl up her arm, or immersing herself briefly in thought. Here she sits in the taiga, far removed from the bustling day-to-day life of cities and nations, far removed from wars and all the troubles of the civilised world. But what if she actually knows this science of imagery to perfection? What if she can use it to influence people and society, and in a more powerful way than all our governments, parliaments and religious denominations? Incredible! A fantasy! But...

There are actual concrete facts which confirm this. Incredible facts, indeed! But they really do exist.

In a very short time she taught me to write books. She needed only three days to do this. She was the one pouring forth over and over again an unending stream of information. Incredible, but fact. Without so much as an advertising campaign, her books have easily spread across municipal and national boundaries. Her image is in these books. By some unknown means this image influences people and arouses creative impulses in them. Thousands of lines of poetry and hundreds of bards' songs are dedicated to her image.

And this is something she has known about all along! Right there in the first book I outlined what she said on this subject. Back then there was nothing as yet. At the time her words seemed like incredible nonsense, like a fantasy. But everything came about exactly as she had said. And now, even as I am writing these lines, incredible things have been happening.

In 1999 the Prof-Press publishing house put out a 500-page anthology of readers' letters and poems.[2] The anthology was published in July, considered a 'dead season' for booksellers. But an incredible thing happened: the whole print-run of 15,000 copies sold out within a single month.

Another 15,000 copies have been printed, but these books instantly sold out, too. Such an event may not be so spectacular for a sensationalism-ridden press. In fact, it goes far beyond the conceptual bounds of sensationalism by virtue of the uniqueness of the conclusions stemming from it — conclusions that defy credulity. It is indeed hard to believe that

---

[2]This readers' anthology, entitled *V luche Anastasii zvuchit dusha Rossii* (The soul of Russia sings in Anastasia's ray), was first released in 1999 by Prof-Press in the city of Rostov-on-Don, and was subsequently re-published by Dilya Publishers of St Petersburg.

Anastasia's image is actually changing the consciousness of society.

Readers feel the need of taking action. People both in Russia and abroad are independently organising readers' clubs and centres, calling them after her.

A Novosibirsk medical factory is producing the cedar oil she talked about. And in a small village in the Novosibirsk Region local residents are repairing their old equipment and endeavouring to produce healing oil according to the technology she recommended, and they are getting help from the city.

It was she herself who said that Siberian villages would be regenerated, and that children would start coming back to their parents.

She has been redirecting the flood of pilgrims from foreign temples to our native sacred sites. In the past two years alone the dolmens she spoke about on the outskirts of Gelendzhik[3] have been visited by over fifty thousand of her readers. Around these previously neglected sacred sites people are now planting flowers and gardens. And in a number of cities they are planting cedars and other growing things according to her method.

By decree of the head of the Tomsk Region administration an enterprise has been set up under the name of *Sibirskie dikorosy* (Siberian Flora). It has now sent four thousand cedar saplings to Moscow.

Scientists are talking about Anastasia. Her image as a living, self-sufficient substance is already soaring across Russia. But only Russia? Women in Kazakhstan are collecting money to make a film about Anastasia. Wow! Here are Kazakh women wanting to make a film about a Siberian recluse?!

---

[3]*dolmens, Gelendzhik* — see footnotes 1 and 2 in Book 1, Chapter 30: "Author's message to readers".

This image of hers is beginning to lead people somewhere. But where? By what power? Who is helping her? It is possible she herself possesses some kind of incredible power hitherto unknown. But why is she staying in her glade as before, still messing about with bugs?

While intellectuals are arguing over whether or not she exists at all, she is simply taking action. The results of her actions can be seen, touched and tasted. What is this science of imagery?

Back in the taiga, I found such thoughts a trifle confusing. I wanted to have them either disproved or confirmed on the spot, but she was the only one around, the only one I could ask.

So I'm going to ask her. She is incapable of lying. I'm going to ask her.

"Tell me, Anastasia... Tell me, do you have a perfect knowledge of the science of imagery? Do you possess the knowledge of those ancient priests?"

I was greatly excited as I awaited her reply, but a calm voice responded without the least hint of excitement:

"I know what my forefather taught those priests. And also what the priests did not give him the opportunity to say. And I have endeavoured to find out and feel new things on my own."

"Now I get it! Just as I thought! You are more of an expert than anyone else on the science of imagery. And you have created your own image and placed it before people. For many you are a goddess, a messiah, a forest sprite. That is how readers write about you in their letters. You have told me I should write down everything — as though pride and self-conceit were a great sin. And I have presented myself before the public as a bumbler, while *you* have come out exalted over everyone, and what's more, you knew it was going to turn out this way in advance."

"Vladimir, I have not concealed anything from you."

Anastasia rose from the ground and stood in front of me, her arms down by her sides. She looked me straight in the eye and went on:

"Only my image is not yet clear to everyone. But that other image which will be out there before the people, will also be mine. My image will resemble that of a cleaning lady who is simply dusting the cobwebs off the most important thing."

"What's this about cobwebs? Speak more clearly, Anastasia. What is it you want to 'create' this time?"

"I want to animate, bring alive, the image of God to people. I want to make His grand dream clear to everyone, so that every living person may feel His aspiration of love. Man can become happy here and now, in this life. The children of people on the Earth today will live in His Paradise. I am not alone. You are not alone. And Paradise will appear as a conjoint co-creation."

"Hold on, hold on there. I realise now that your words will cause many teachings to fall apart. Their instigators and their followers will start not only lambasting you but bombarding me too. Who needs problems like that? I refuse to write down everything you say about God."

"Vladimir, here you are afraid just of the thought of struggling with someone you do not know."

"No, it's all quite clear to me. I'll get descended upon by all the religious leaders. They'll poison their fanatical followers against me."

"It is not *them* — you are afraid of *yourself,* Vladimir. You are ashamed to present yourself before God. You do not believe in your new way of life. You think you cannot change."

"What's this got to do with me? I'm telling you about the clerics. So many of them are already reacting to your sayings."

"And what are they saying to you?" Anastasia enquired.

"Different things. Some react negatively, while others — just the opposite. One Orthodox priest from Ukraine came to me along with his parishioners in support of your sayings. But he's just a country priest."

"And what do you mean when you say a 'country' priest came to see you?"

"I mean there are others, higher-ups. Everybody's subject to them. Everything depends on them."

"But still, even those 'higher-ups', as you call them, also once served in the smaller churches."

"That makes no difference. All the same I'm not going to write until at least somebody in charge of some major temple... Anyway, what am I saying? You can predict everything that's going to happen ahead of time. So tell me, who will be against you, and who will help you? Will there be anyone, in fact, who comes to your assistance?"

"What clerical rank could convince you to be bolder, Vladimir?"

"Nothing less than a Father Superior or a bishop. Can you name any?"

She thought just for a split-second, as though gazing into both time and space at once.

And then came this incredible answer:

"Assistance has already come, Vladimir, from someone who has uttered new statements about God — namely Pope John Paul II," Anastasia replied. "The images of Christ and Mohammed will unite their energies in space, and other images will merge together with them. There will also be an Orthodox patriarch,[4] whose words will be revered for centuries. But, most importantly, there will be impulses of inspiration among all ordinary people. It may be their earthly status that

---

[4]*patriarch* — the titular head of the Russian Orthodox Church.

is important to you, but, after all, *truth* is more important than anything on Earth."

At this point Anastasia ceased talking and lowered her eyes, as though she had been suddenly offended by something. It appeared as though a lump in her throat had welled up, but she swallowed it and sighed. Then she added:

"Forgive me — I fear I am not making myself clear to your heart. Things are not working out at the moment on my part, but I shall try to be clearer, only let the people hear..."

"About what?"

"About what others have tried for a thousand years to hide from them. About how it takes hardly a moment for any one of them to enter the Creator's pristine garden and there bring about splendid conjoint creations with Him."

I could feel a sense of agitation building inside her. And I myself, for some reason, began feeling agitated, and said:

"Don't be concerned. Tell me, Anastasia, and perhaps I *shall* be able to understand and write about it."

And what she went on to say she said in an extremely concrete and simple way. It was only later, after analysing and pondering her words, that I began to understand, and could feel some sense — a significant sense at that — in her words "Take back your Motherland, people!" But back there, in the forest, I asked her once more:

"I see how it's all going to come about. I see that if you can so easily bring out images of life of thousands of years ago, that means you must know all religious teachings and treatises, and that you will reveal them to people?"

"I know the teachings that called forth reverence among people."

"All of them?"

"Yes, all of them."

"And the Vedic scriptures you can translate in their entirety?"

"I can. Only why waste time on that?"

"But look, don't you want mankind to know about those ancient teachings? Tell me about them, and I shall write about them in my next book."

"And what then? What do you think will be the net benefit to mankind?"

"What d'you mean? They'll become wiser."

"Vladimir, the whole nature of the dark forces' trap is that with their multitude of teachings they try to conceal the most important thing from Man. By presenting a portion of truth — only for the mind — in their treatises, they deliberately lead people away from the most important thing."

"Then why do people call the ones that present such teachings *wise men?*"

"Vladimir, if you will allow me, I shall tell you a parable. It is a parable that a thousand years ago was whispered by wise men to each other in some secluded spot. For many centuries now no one has heard this parable."

"Then go ahead and tell it to me, if you think that the parable may be helpful in explaining something."

CHAPTER TWENTY-FIVE

Two brothers
(A parable)

Once upon a time lived a couple that for many years had no children. When they were well on in age, the wife bore twin boys — two brothers. The labour was difficult, and shortly after childbirth their mother passed on to the next world.

Their father hired wet-nurses, and tried to bring up his children as best he could. And he managed indeed, for nigh on fourteen years. But as his boys approached their fifteenth birthday, the father himself passed on.

After burying their father, the two brothers sat mourning in their room. Two twin brothers. Three minutes separated their emergings into the world, and so between the two of them one was considered the elder, his brother the younger. After a period of mournful silence the elder brother spoke:

"Our father on his deathbed told us of his sorrow that he had not been able to impart to us the wisdom of life. How shall you and I live without wisdom, my dear younger brother? Without wisdom our family line will go on in misery. People who have managed to gain wisdom from their fathers might laugh at us."

"Do not be sad," said the younger to his elder brother. "You spend a good deal of time in reverie. Perchance time will afford you the opportunity in your reverie to learn wisdom too. I shall do everything you say. I myself can live without reverie, yet I still find living a pleasing experience. I am happy when the day dawns and when it draws to a close. I shall simply live, take care of the household, while you are learning wisdom."

"Agreed," replied the elder to the younger. "Only there is no opportunity to seek out wisdom by staying here at home. There is no wisdom here, no one has left it here and no one will bring it to us of their own accord. But I as the elder brother have decided I must, for both our sakes, and for the sake of our line which will extend through time, find everything that is wise in this world. I must find it and bring it home, and bestow it upon our descendants as well as our own selves. I shall take with me everything of value our father left us, and travel throughout the world and meet all the wise people of different lands. I shall learn all their teachings and then return to my native home."

"Your course will be a long one," said the younger brother sympathetically. "We have a horse. Take the horse, and the cart as well, and on your departure take along as much goods as you can carry, so that you will find your journey the less hard. I shall stay at home and await your returning as the wisest of men."

The brothers parted for a very long time. Years went by. The elder brother went from wise man to wise man, from temple to temple, learning the teachings of the Orient and the Occident, journeying to the North and to the South. He possessed a colossal memory, and his keen intellect quickly grasped everything he heard and committed it to heart.

For about sixty years the elder brother plied the highways and byways of the world. His hair and beard turned to ashen grey. His inquisitive mind kept roaming and honing his wisdom. And this ageing pilgrim came to be considered himself the wisest of men. He was followed around by a crowd of disciples. To inquisitive minds he generously preached his wisdom. Both young and old hung on his every word. And his glory and fame preceded him wherever he came, and communities would proclaim in advance the wise man's great coming.

And so it was in an aura of glory, surrounded by a throng of obsequious disciples, that the ageing wise man drew nearer and nearer to the village where he was born and the house which he had left sixty years before as a youth of fifteen.

All the people of the village turned out to greet him, and the younger brother, showing similar signs of grey, ran toward him rejoicing, and bowed his head before his learned brother. And he whispered with gladsome tenderness:

"Bless me, O my learned brother. Come into our home, I shall wash your feet after your long journey. Come into our home, my wise brother, and take your rest."

With a magnanimous sweep of his hand he gestured to all his disciples to remain on the little hill in front of the village, accept gifts from the well-wishers and engage in learned conversations, while he himself entered the home of his younger brother. The wise man, like an ageing dignitary, sat down wearily at the table in the spacious upper room. And the younger brother began washing his feet with warm water and listening to what his learned brother had to say. And the wise man began speaking to him as follows:

"I have fulfilled my duty. I have learnt the teachings of the great wise men of the Earth, and I have created teachings of my own. I shall not stay long at home. Now to impart what I have learnt to others — that is my part. But since I promised to bring my wisdom home, I shall fulfil my promise and sojourn a day or two with you. During this extent of time, my dear younger brother, I shall impart to you the wisest pearls of truth in the world.

"Here is the first: *all people should live in a splendid garden.*"

Drying his elder brother's feet with a beautifully embroidered towel, the younger went to considerable effort to please him, saying:

"Go to, my brother. On the table before you are the fruits of our garden — I have gathered the very best for you."

The wise man thoughtfully tasted the marvellous array of fruits before him, and went on:

"*Every Man living on the Earth should cultivate his own family tree.* When he dies, the tree will remain as a good memorial for his descendants. It will purify the air with its leaves so that his descendants will be better able to breathe. We should all be able to breathe good air."

The younger brother began to show signs of haste and effort, and said:

"Forgive me, my wise brother, I forgot to open the window so that you can breathe fresh air." Whereupon he threw the window open and then went on:

"Here, breathe the air of our two cedar trees. I planted them the year you left. I dug a hole with my spade for one of the saplings, for the other I used the spade you played with when we were youngsters."

The wise man thoughtfully gazed at the trees, and then intoned:

"Love is a grand feeling. Not everyone is handed the opportunity to live his life with love. And there is a grand wisdom: *each of us should strive every day for love.*"

"Oh, how wise you are, my dear elder brother!" exclaimed the younger. "You have learnt such great wisdom, and I am embarrassed in your presence. Forgive me, I have not even introduced you to my wife..." And he called out toward the doorway:

"*Starushka!* Where are you, my little cookie?"[1]

"Here I am!" a voice piped up. And in the doorway a cheerful old woman appeared with plates of fresh steaming pies in her hands. "Sorry, I've been busy making pies."

---

[1] *starushka* — an affectionate term for an elderly woman; *little cookie* (Russian: *striapushka*) — an endearing name derived from the word *striapukha* (lit., 'cook'), and rhyming with *starushka*.

Putting the pies down on the table, the cheerful *starushka* did a playful curtsy to the two brothers. And then she went over to the younger brother, her husband, and whispered in his ear, but loudly enough for the elder brother to hear:

"And now you must forgive me, hubby, I have to go lie down."

"How now, my ne'er-do-well?" her husband replied. "You've decided to go have a nap when we have an honoured guest? My very own brother — and you go...?"

"It's not that, my head is spinning and I'm starting to feel a bit nauseous."

"And how could that possibly happen to you, my little busy-body?"

"Perhaps you are the one to blame, no doubt, again. I am once more with child," laughed the *starushka,* as she ran off.

"My apologies, brother," the younger brother excused himself in some embarrassment. "She doesn't know the value of wisdom, she's always been light-hearted and is still that way, even in her old age."

The wise man's thoughtful moments became increasingly longer. His reverie was broken by the sound of children's voices. The wise man heard them and said:

"Every Man should strive to learn great wisdom. *To learn how to raise children that will be happy and righteous.*"

"Tell me, learned brother, I long to make my children and grandchildren happy — you see, my noisy little grandchildren have just come in."

Two boys no older than six and a little girl of about four were standing in the doorway and quarrelling amongst themselves. In an attempt to smooth things out, the grey-haired younger brother hastened to say to them:

"Quickly tell me what all the fuss is about, my noisy ones. You're interfering in our conversation."

"Oh," the smaller boy exclaimed, "it seems our one grandpa has become two! Well then now, which is ours and which is not, how do we tell?"

"Here's our Grandpakins sitting right here, isn't it clear?" piped up the little girl, running over to the younger brother, putting her cheek against his leg, tousling his beard and prattling:

"Grandpakins, Grandpakins, I was coming to see you all by myself, to show you how I've learnt to dance, and the boys decided to tag along all on their own. One of them wants to draw with you — see, he's brought a board and some chalk. The other's brought a flute and a pipe — he wants you to play them for him. But Grandpakins, Grandpakins, I was the one who decided to come and see you first. You tell the others that. You can send them home, Grandpakins!"

"She's wrong. I came first to draw with you, and my brother only then decided he wanted to come with me, to play the flute," observed the boy carrying the thin piece of board.

"There are two of you grandpakins, you decide," the granddaughter chimed in. "Which of us came first? You'd better decide that I was first, or else I'm going to feel terribly hurt and cry."

The wise man smiled sadly at the youngsters. He furrowed his brow, working out a response in his mind, but said nothing. The younger brother became flustered, and decided to cut short the ensuing pause. He took the flute out of his grandson's hands and said without stopping to think:

"We don't have any cause for quarrel here. Dance, my pretty little jumper, and I shall accompany your dance on the flute. My dear little musician will accompany me on the pipe. And you, my dear little artist, draw what the sounds of the music are drawing, and draw the ballerina doing her dance. And now, everybody to their tasks — look to it, lads!"

Whereupon the younger brother struck up a cheerful and splendid melody on the flute, and the grandchildren enthusiastically imitated him in time, portraying their favourite images. The future famous musician playing the pipe tried his best to keep up with the melody. The blushing girl leapt about like a ballerina in a delightful portrayal of her dance. The future artist drew a picture full of joy.

The wise man kept silent. The wise man realised... When the merriment was finished, he rose and said solemnly:

"You remember, my dear younger brother, our father's old hammer and chisel. Give them to me, and I shall hew out on a rock the most important lesson of all. Then I shall go away. I probably shan't come back. Don't stop me, and don't wait for me."

The elder brother left. The ageing wise man went with his disciples over to a great rock which a pathway bent around. The same pathway that lured wisdom-seeking pilgrims into lands far from home. A whole day passed, and night fell, but the grey-haired wise man kept hammering and chiselling away at the inscription on the rock. When the aged man finished his work in exhaustion, his disciples read the inscription on the rock:

Whatever you seek, pilgrim, you are already carrying with you. You keep losing it with every step you take, and are finding nothing new.

Upon finishing the parable, Anastasia fell silent. She gave me an enquiring look in the eye, no doubt wondering what I had got from it.

"Well, Anastasia, I took from the parable that all the pearls of wisdom the elder brother talked about, the younger brother was already implementing in his day-to-day life. There's just one thing that isn't clear to me, though: who taught the younger brother all these wise things?"

"No one. All the wisdom of the Universe is included for ever in each soul right from the moment it is created. It is just that wise men slyly intellectualise for their own interests, and thereby lead people away from the most important thing."

"From 'the most important thing'? But what *is* the most important thing?"

CHAPTER TWENTY-SIX

Even today everyone
can build a home

"The most important thing, Vladimir, is that even today everyone can build a home. Everyone can feel God with their soul and live in Paradise. One single moment is all that separates Paradise from people living on the Earth today. Each one possesses conscious awareness within. When dogmas do not interfere with this awareness, then look, Vladimir, what can come to pass..."

All at once Anastasia brightened. She grasped hold of my hand and led me to the shore of the lake where there was a patch of bare sand, and started talking to me along the way.

"It only takes a moment. You will understand everything in just a moment of time. And everyone will understand — the readers, yours and mine.

"Within themselves they will define the essence of the Earth, and become aware of their destined purpose. Right this moment, Vladimir, see, right this moment we shall in our thoughts build our home! I and you, and all of them too. And I assure you indeed that the thought of each one of them will be brought into contact with the thought of God. The gates of Paradise will open. Let us go, let us move with more speed. I shall draw it with a stick upon the shore...

"We shall build a home together with those who into contact with your written words will later come. All human thought will merge together into one. Believe me, people have God's ability within them to turn what they conceive into reality. And many a home will stand upon the land. And each one in their own homes will be able to grasp everything first hand. They will be able to feel and understand the aspirations of the Divine dream. We shall build a home! I and you, and all of them too!"

"Hold on there, Anastasia. There are a whole bunch of different designs out there for homes where people are living now. What sense can there be in proposing yet another one?"

"Vladimir, you must do more than simply listen to me! You must feel everything that I outline, and mentally complete yourself the whole design, and let everyone else draw it along with me. O, God! People, at least give it a try, I beg of you!"

Anastasia was literally trembling with joyful excitement. She was reaching out to people, and I found myself growing more and more interested in her design. And at first it seemed simple to me, yet at the same time I had the feeling as though this recluse, Anastasia, was revealing to everyone a most extraordinary secret. The whole secret was in utter simplicity, and if I can remember the events in order, this is how they all went.

Anastasia continued:

"First choose for yourself a place of your own you like best of all the pleasing spaces on the Earth. A place where you would like to live, and would like your children to live out their lives. And then you will indeed leave to your great-grandchildren a fitting memorial to you. The climate, too, in that place must be favourable for you. Take one hectare[1] of land in that place for yourself in perpetuity."

"But nobody can just come along and take any piece of land they jolly well desire. Land today is sold only in places where people wish to sell it."

---

[1]*hectare* — designating an area 100 metres square or 10,000 square metres, approximately equivalent to 2.5 acres in the Imperial system.

"Yes, unfortunately, everything happens that way today. Our Motherland is extensive, but there is not a single hectare of your land where you can create a corner of Paradise for your children and descendants. And yet the time has now come when we must begin acting on this cause. And take advantage of the most favourable of all the existing laws."

"I don't know all the laws, of course, but I'm sure there is no law allowing someone to take possession of a parcel of land in perpetuity. Farmers can rent a good deal of land, but only for ninety-nine years."[2]

"Well then, we can start by taking it for a shorter span of time, but we need at once to plan a law so that everyone may have his own parcel of ground, his own Motherland. Whether or not and to what degree the country flourishes as a state depends on this. And if there is no appropriate law at the moment, well, you will have to make one."

"That's easier said than done. Our laws are made by the State Duma. It has to make some amendment or introduce a new article into the Constitution. And the parties in the Duma are constantly fighting with each other — there's no way they can settle the land question."

"Then if there is no party capable of enshrining into law everyone's right to their Motherland, you will have to form such a party."[3]

---

[2] *ninety-nine years* — Ninety-nine-year leases, still in effect in Russia, were once common in many lands. Yet even today, the right to so-called 'land ownership' in most Western countries can be all too easily abrogated by governments if taxes on the land are not paid (and paid on time!), or if 'private' land is expropriated for a deemed 'public' need (the legal doctrine of *eminent domain*).

[3] *a party* — In 2005 the Russian 'Motherland party' (*Rodnaya partiya*) was established with the specific purpose of bringing forth legislation on allocating 'pieces of Motherland' to people in the form of family plots, just as Anastasia proposes here. In fact, the name *Rodnaya partiya* was suggested in Book 8 (Part 2) of the Ringing Cedars Series, published shortly before the new party was announced.

"And who will set it up?"

"Those who will read about the home we are creating and become aware of what a Motherland means to each one, to each Man living today, and to the future of the whole Earth."

"Well, enough about political parties. Tell me rather about this unusual home of yours. I'm really interested now in what new design you can possibly bring forth. Let's say someone has come into possession of a hectare of land. Not exactly a Paradise, but, say, one grown over with wild grasses — they're probably not going to give him better than that. And there he is, standing on his hectare of land — what next?"

"Think about it yourself, Vladimir, and dream a little, too. What could you do if you were standing on your own land?"

Chapter Twenty-Seven

A fence

"First of all," I said, "first of all, everything, of course, must be enclosed by a fence. Otherwise, when they start bringing in building materials to construct the manor house, somebody could come along and pilfer them. And when you plant a crop, it might be stolen before you harvest it. Or are you against fences on principle?"

"I am not against them, Vladimir. Even animals mark out their own territory. Only what are you going to make the fence of?"

"What d'you mean, what of? Fence boards, of course... No, wait. Fence boards can turn out to be on the expensive side. For starters you need to dig post holes and string up barbed wire all around the property. Even then you should still put up boards so people wouldn't see inside the fence."

"And how many years could a board fence last without needing repair?"

"If it is constructed of good material, if you keep it painted or varnished and smear the parts of the posts that are in the ground with pitch, it might go five years or more without needing repair."

"And then?"

"Then you'd probably need to do some repair work and touch it up to keep it from rotting."

"So, that means you will constantly have to fuss over the fence. And it will give your children and grandchildren even greater cause for concern. Would it not be better to construct it so your children will not have to bother about it, and so that their view will not be spoilt by the sight of rotting timber? Let us think how to make the fence more solid and long-lasting, so that your descendants may have fonder remembrances of you."

"Of course, you can build it so it will last longer. Who wouldn't want that? For example, you could make brick pillars and a brick foundation, and put cast-iron grill work in between — that kind of fence doesn't rust. It can even last a hundred years. But only very rich people can afford to build a fence like that. Can you imagine? A whole hectare — that's a perimeter of 400 metres. A fence like that's going to set you back several hundred thousand roubles, maybe even millions. Still, it'll last a good hundred years, maybe two hundred or more. You can even have it made with all sorts of family monograms. Your descendants will look at it and remember their great-grandfather, and it'll be the envy of everyone around."

"Envy is not a good feeling, Vladimir. In fact, it is harmful."

"Well, there's not much you can do about that. I tell you, enclosing a hectare of land with a good fence is not something many people can afford."

"That means we must think up some other kind of fence."

"What other kind? Can you suggest something?"

"Would it not be better, Vladimir, in place of a whole lot of posts, which can later rot, to plant trees?"

"Trees? And then what, nail boards...?"

"Why nail boards to them? Look there, in the forest there are a lot of trees growing with their trunks only one-and-one-half to two metres apart."

"Yes, you're right. But there are holes between them. It's not the same as a fence."

"But it is possible to plant bushes in between them that people cannot get through. Take a careful look, and think what a splendid living fence you would have! And it would

be just a little bit different with each person. And everyone
would come to admire the view. And your descendants in
the ages to come will remember the creator of this splendid
hedge. And the hedge will not only save them time on repairs
but will bring them benefits as well. It will serve, in fact, as far
more than just a barrier. One person will make a hedge out of
birches growing in a row. Another will use oak. And someone
with a creative impulse will make a coloured hedge, the kind
one reads about in fairy tales."

"What d'you mean, coloured?"

"Planting different-coloured trees. Birches, maples, oaks
and cedars. Someone may intertwine a rowan-tree with clusters of bright red berries and still plant guelder-roses in between. And make room for bird-cherry trees and lilac bushes. After all, you can plan it all out in advance. Each planter
should watch to see how high each one grows, how it blooms
in the spring, what kind of a fragrance it has and what feath-
ered friends it attracts. Thus your hedge will be both sono-
rous and pleasantly fragrant, and you will never get tired of
looking at it, as the picture will be changing its tints with each
passing day. It will flourish with colours anew every spring
and every autumn burst forth in an explosion of fiery hues."

"Well, Anastasia, it seems you're a poetess as well. We began with just a simple fence, and now see what all you've made
of it! You know, I really like the way you've turned the whole
thing around. And why haven't people thought of this before?
No painting required, no repair. And when the trees get too
big, they can be cut down and used for firewood and people
can plant new trees — they can change the picture, just like
an artist. The only thing is, won't it take a long time to plant
that kind of a hedge? And if you're going to plant the trees
two metres apart, then you've got to dig two hundred holes
for the saplings. And then plant the bushes in between. And
no technology will be allowed, you'll say."

"On the contrary, Vladimir. There is no sense in rejecting technology for the project at hand. Indeed, any invention of the dark forces must be put to use to serve the forces of light. It will hasten the implementation of the plan if you use a plough to dig a trench around the perimeter of the ground-lot and plant the saplings in it, along with the seeds at the same time — for the bushes you have decided to plant between the trees. Then you can go over it again with the plough to fill in the soil. While the earth is still loose, you can adjust the position of each sapling to even out the row."

"That's fantastic. So in two or three days one person can put in a whole hedge."

"Yes."

"The only drawback is that until the hedge grows, it won't deter any thieves. And people will have to wait a long time for it to grow. Especially in the case of oak and cedar."

"But birch and aspen grow quickly, and the bushes between them will not take much time either. If you are in a hurry, you can plant tree saplings two metres high right away. When the birches are grown, they can be cut up for household use, and their places will be taken by the maturing cedar and oak trees."

"Okay, then, a living fence is something I can grasp. I really like it. Now tell me, what style of house do you see on the ground-lot?"

"Perhaps we should first plan out the lot as a whole, Vladimir?"

"What d'you have in mind — different beds for tomatoes, potatoes, cucumbers? That's usually women's work. House-building is a man's job. I think you need to build one large house right off — a fashionable manor house in the European style so that your grandchildren and great-grandchildren will remember you fondly. Then there can be a smaller cottage for the servants. It's a pretty big lot, after all. It'll require a lot of work."

"Vladimir, if everything is done properly from the start, there will be no need for servants. Everything around you will serve you with great pleasure and with love — and not only you but your children and whole family, and your grand-children too."

"It doesn't happen that way with anyone. Even with your beloved dachniks.[1] They only have five or six hundred square metres, yet they're working it every free day from dawn 'til dusk. And here they're going to have a whole hectare! It's going to take at least a dozen dump-trucks every year just to bring in the fertiliser and manure.

"First the loads of manure have to be spread over the whole growing area, and then all the earth has to be dug up and turned over. Otherwise nothing will grow right. And you'd better add some kind of fertiliser — you can get it in special stores. If you don't fertilise, the soil won't give a good yield. It's something agronomists — people who study agri-culture — know and dachniks have learnt from experience. I hope you agree on the need for fertiliser."

"Of course, the earth needs fertilising, but the task need not be devitalising. God has thought through everything in advance so that the ground in the place you wish to live will turn out to have the right nutrients and be in an ideal con-dition without wearisome physical efforts on your part. You need only make contact with His thought and feel the whole-ness of the system He has designed, instead of just relying on your own intellect in making decisions."

"Then why is nothing fertilised today, anywhere on the Earth, according to God's system?"

[1]*dachniks* — people who spend time (their days off, especially summer holidays) tending a garden at their *dacha,* or cottage in the country. See further details in Book 1.

Above: A raspberry 'living fence' grown by Sergei and Vera Bondar, Nizhny Novgorod, Russia. In addition to producing abundant harvests of raspberries, this maintenance-free hedge protects the garden from winds, attracts birds that naturally control pests and keeps unwanted visitors out. Photo © 2004 by Alexey Kondaurov.

Below: Kin's domain design © 2003 by Irina Labountsova, *Zapolyanie* eco-village. In response to Anastasia's plea, thousands of people all across Russia and beyond have created designs of their family domains and started turning them into reality.

"Vladimir, you must do more than simply listen to me! You must feel everything that I outline, and mentally complete yourself the whole design, and let everyone else draw it along with me. O, God! People, at least give it a try, I beg of you!"

— *Anastasia's words from Ch. 26: "Even today everyone can build a home"*

Opposite page: Plan of the *Solnyshko* ('Sunshine') community composed of kin's domains (top). Marina Detner's kin's domain (bottom).

This page: kin's domains of Marina (top) and Dima & Julia (bottom).

All drawings © 2003 Raduga Centre, Murmansk.

"We shall build a home together with those who into contact with your written words will later come. All human thought will merge together into one. Believe me, people have God's ability within them to turn what they conceive into reality. And many a home will stand upon the land." — *Ch. 26: "Even today everyone can build a home"*

True to Anastasia's promise, new homes have sprouted all across Russia as thousands of people, inspired by her dream, start to lay foundations for their family domains or bring dying villages back to life.

This page & opposite page, top: new homes & residents of the *Rodnoe* eco-village, Vladimir Region, © Leonid Sharashkin, 2004–2006. *Opposite page, bottom:* flourishing gardens in the *Podgornoe* village (*Raduzhie* community), Republic of Mariy El, Russia, attract visitors to a permaculture workshop, August 2006, © Alexey Kondaurov, 2006.

Mixed permaculture plantings in Vasiliy and Marina's garden, *Raduzhie* community (*Podgornoe* village), Republic of Mariy El, Russia, © Alexey Kondaurov, 2006. Like millions of other food-gardeners throughout Russia, this family uses no chemical fertilisers or pesticides, yet manages to grow abundant harvests in a climate with a growing season of only 110 days. According to official statistics, in 2005 Russian gardeners, using less than 3% of the country's agricultural land, produced over 53% of the nation's agricultural output — more than all the commercial producers taken together.

Above: a 'build-your-home wonder-cake', representing a small-scale model of a kin's domain complete with a 'living fence' and garden plantings, becomes a festive table centrepiece in the *Kovcheg* eco-village, Kaluga Region, during a celebration on 16 September 2006. *Below:* young girls in search for their intended mate set small rafts afloat during a 'Find-your-soulmate' festival in the *Rodovoe* eco-community, Tula Region, 20 June 2006. For a description of this ancient ritual and its significance, see Chapter 5 in Book 6 of the Ringing Cedars Series. Photos © 2006 Alexey Kondaurov, Nizhny Novgorod.

Dachnik Day celebration at the *Rodnoe* eco-village, Vladimir Region, 23 July 2006. Residents of *Rodnoe* and nearby eco-villages, along with numerous guests, share greens, vegetables and fruit they have grown themselves on their plots. The Dachnik Day holiday — proposed in Book 2 of the Ringing Cedars Series to honour the millions of gardeners and celebrate Man's connectedness to the Earth — is now celebrated by thousands of individuals, families and communities throughout Russia and beyond. Photo © 2006 by Leonid Sharashkin.

"Vladimir, right now you are in the taiga. Look around you, how high the trees are, how mighty their trunks! Among the trees herbs and bushes are growing. There are raspberries, and currants... indeed, a whole lot of everything grows right here in the taiga for Man's use. And over thousands of years not a single person has fertilised the ground. But the land remains fruitful. What do you think: how has it been fertilised and by whom?"

"By whom? I don't know how or by whom. But you've pointed out a really important fact. Indeed, it's simply amazing how Man somehow gets everything twisted around. Tell me yourself, why aren't various kinds of fertiliser needed in the taiga?"

"Here in the taiga God's thought and God's plan are not interfered with to the same degree as where Man lives today. In the taiga leaves fall from the trees, and little branches are torn off by the breeze. And these leaves and branches, along with worms, fertilise the ground in the taiga. And the grass which grows all around regulates the composition of the earth. The bushes help it clear away excesses of acids and alkalis. None of the fertilisers you are familiar with can substitute for leaves falling from the trees. After all, leaves include many of the diverse energies of the Universe. They have seen the stars, the Sun and the Moon. And not only seen, but they have interacted with them. And even many thousands of years from now, the ground here in the taiga will still be fertile."

"But the ground-lot where our house is to be built is not the taiga, you see."

"Then start planning! You yourself can plant a forest of different kinds of trees."

"Anastasia, maybe it'd be best if you told me right off how to make it so that the soil on the plot stays fertilised all on its own? That is a major undertaking, since there are so many other things to do. Planting beds, warding off various kinds of pests..."

"Of course we could talk about details and particulars, but it would be best for each one to apply his own thought, his soul and his dream to the building work. Each of us knows instinctively what will be the most suitable arrangement for him and bring joy to his children and grandchildren. There can be no one single plan that fits all. Each plan is individual, like a great artist's masterpiece. Each Man must make it his own."

"But give me an example. At least tell me in general terms."

"All right — look, I shall do a little outlining for you. But first there is the most important thing to understand. Everything is created by God's hand for the good of Man. You are a Man and can control everything around you. You are a Man! Try to comprehend and feel through your soul what constitutes a real Paradise on the Earth..."

"Now more specifically, Anastasia, without philosophising. Tell me what to plant and where, tell me where I should dig. What cash crops should I grow that will bring me the biggest return on my investment?"

"Vladimir, do you know why peasants and farmers today are so unhappy?"

"Well no, why?"

"So many of them are striving to bring in as big a harvest as they can. To sell. They think more about money than about the land. They themselves do not believe they can be happy in their own family nest, they think the rest of the people are happy in the big cities. Believe me, Vladimir, whatever is created in your soul will unfailingly be reflected in the whole world around you.

"Of course, outward details are also necessary. Let us think together about one way we can plan out our plot. I shall simply start things rolling, and you help me on your part."

"Okay, I'll help. You start."

"Let us say our lot is on a barren section of land, and is now enclosed on all sides by a hedge. Let us divide it, reserving half or three-quarters of the lot for a forest, and there plant a variety of trees. On the edge of the forest, where it borders on the remaining part of the lot, we shall plant a hedge in such a way that animals cannot pass through it and trample the crops growing in the garden plot.

"In the forest we shall set up a pen using densely planted saplings, which in time will be home to a goat or two. And we shall also use saplings to construct a shelter for egg-laying hens.

"In the garden plot we shall make a pond approximately 16 metres across. We shall plant raspberry and currant bushes among the trees in the forest, and wild strawberries around the edge. Later, after the trees in the forest have grown a little, we can set up two or three empty log hives there for bees. And we shall use trees to make a gazebo where you will have a cool place, safe from the heat, to talk with your children or your friends. And we can make a summer sleeping area out of living things, along with a creative workshop for you. And sleeping places for the children, and a living room."

"Wow! It won't be a forest we end up with, but more of a palace!"

"Only the palace will be a living entity, and continue to grow in perpetuity. This is how the Creator Himself thought up the whole balance of things. And all Man has to do is to assign everything its task — according to his own taste, design and understanding."

"But why didn't the Creator do it all this way to begin with? Everything in the forest grows just where it happens to end up."

"Think of the forest as a book for you as a creator. Look more closely, Vladimir — everything therein has been written by the Father. Look over there: three trees are growing just a half-metre apart. You are free to plant them in a row and use a whole lot of them to make up other configurations. In among the trees there are bushes growing — think of how you can make use of them to sweeten your life. And where the trees do not allow grass and bushes to grow between them, you can take that as a lesson for building your future house out of living materials. It is as though all you have to do is to formulate the required programme and adjust it according to your taste. Everything around you is charged with the task of cherishing and delighting you and your children, cherishing and feeding them."

"To feed ourselves, we'll need to plant a vegetable garden. And that'll take a lot of sweat."

"Believe me, Vladimir, even the vegetable garden can be set up so that it will not be an aggravation. You just need to keep everything under observation. Among the herbs, just the way everything grows in the forest, you could have the most splendid tomatoes and cucumbers under cultivation. Their taste will be much more appealing and healthful for the body than when they are grown simply on a patch of bare ground."

"But what about the weeds? And won't they be destroyed by pests and beetles?"

"There is nothing useless in Nature, Vladimir, and there are no purposeless weeds. Neither are there any beetles that are harmful to Man."

"What d'you mean, there aren't any harmful beetles?! Take locusts, for example, or the Colorado beetle — a real vermin that eats away at potato crops in the fields."

"Yes, it does. It is also thereby showing people how their ignorance is eating away at the self-sufficiency of the Earth, contradicting the designs of the Divine Creator. How can people keep stubbornly ploughing year after year in one and the same place, torturing the ground? It is like scraping an open wound, at the same time demanding benefits from the wound. Locusts or the Colorado beetle will not touch the ground-lot which you and I have outlined. When everything grows together in one grand harmony, the fruits accruing to the owner are also harmonious."

"But if that's the way everything is going to ultimately turn out, meaning that on the lot you have thought up there is no need for Man to fertilise the ground, or fight off vermin with various kinds of poisons, or do weeding, and everything is just going to grow all by itself, then what is there left for *Man* to do?"

"Live in Paradise. The way God wanted us to. Anyone who is able to build himself a Paradise like that will come into contact with the Divine thought and produce a new co-creation together with Him."

"What new co-creation?"

"Its turn will come once the creation of Paradise has been completed in due course. Let us consider now what you and I still need to do."

CHAPTER TWENTY-EIGHT

Home

"We still have to build ourselves a decent home," I observed. "A place for our children and grandchildren to live, problem-free. A two-storey brick manor house with a toilet, bathroom and hot-water heater. You can do that for any private home these days. I was at a building fair recently and noticed how a lot of different facilities have been developed for conveniences in private homes. Or are you again going to object that we don't need to use any technological gadgets?"

"On the contrary, they are necessary. You need to make everything serve the cause of good as the opportunity presents itself. Besides, it is important that there be a smooth transition in people's habits. Only your grandchildren will not need the kind of home *you* are building. They will understand on their own as they grow up. They will need another kind of home. That is why it is not worthwhile spending too much effort to make the house extremely big or solid."

"Anastasia, I can tell you've got another sly trick up your sleeve. You keep rejecting everything I propose, even the house. I think there is no question but it should be a decent house. You said we would be designing this project together, and here you're thwarting me at every turn, no matter what I say."

"Of course we are doing it together, Vladimir. Besides, I am not rejecting anything, I am simply expressing my views. And each one must decide for himself what comes closest to his own taste."

"You should have told me a little more about your views right off. I don't think anyone's going to understand why the house should not stay the way it is for the grandchildren."

"The other home will still preserve their love for you and their everlasting memories of you. When your grandchildren grow up, they will understand which materials out of all the ones thought up on the Earth will be the most pleasant, solid and useful for them. Right now you do not have those kinds of materials. Your grandchildren will build a wooden house using those trees which their grandfather planted 'way back when' and which their father and mother so loved. That home will start curing them, it will keep them from impurities and inspire them to what is bright. The grand energy of Love will dwell in that home."

"Yes... Interesting... A home made of materials, of the trees cultivated by their grandfather, and their father and mother. And you say it will help protect those living in this home? How? There's some kind of mysticism involved here."

"Why would you call the bright energy of Love 'mysticism', Vladimir?"

"Because not everything's clear to me. Here I've been talking about designing a home and a ground-lot, and now you've all of a sudden started stating things about *love*."

"But why 'all of a sudden'? You have to create everything with love right from the start."

"What — the living fence too? And d'you have to plant the saplings in the forest with love, too?"

"Of course. The grand energy of Love and all the planets in creation will help you lead a full life, a life inherent in a son of God."

"Now you've *really* started talking incomprehensibly, Anastasia. From a house and garden you've gone back to 'God' again. What relation could there possibly be here?"

"Forgive me for not being clearer in my explanation, Vladimir. Allow me to try a different route in trying to explain the significance of our project."

"Go ahead. Only it turns out it's *your* project, not *ours*."

"It belongs to everyone, Vladimir. Many people will sense it intuitively in their hearts. But Man will be prevented from grasping its specific details by fly-by-night dogmas, sounds of the technocratic way of doing things and the many scientific disciplines that are attempting to lead people away from happiness."

"All the more reason for you to try putting everything in more specific terms."

"All right, I shall try. Oh, how I wish my explanations could be clearer to people — oh, how I wish they could! O logic of Divine aspirations, help me choose phrases and word-combinations that will be more clearly understood!"

CHAPTER TWENTY-NINE

The energy of Love

"The great energy of Love is sent to the Earth by God for His children. It comes to each of them at one time or another. It frequently tries to cheer Man with its warmth and stay near him for ever. But most people do not give the great Divine energy the opportunity of remaining with them for long.

"Imagine a couple where he and she meet at one point in the resplendent radiance of love. They endeavour to join their lives together in perpetuity. They consider that their union will be made more solid if affirmed on paper and by ritual in front of a large gathering of witnesses. But all to no avail. It takes but a few days for the energy of Love to fade from their lives. And it happens that way with just about everyone."

"Yes, you are right, Anastasia. A tremendous number of people get divorced. About seventy percent. And it often happens that those who don't get divorced end up living like a dog and cat together, or show complete indifference to each other. Everybody knows this, but nobody can figure out why it happens on such a massive scale. You claim the energy of Love fades from their lives, but why? As though it were some-how aiming to tease everyone or playing some kind of game it's invented?"

"Love does not tease anyone and it does not play games. It tries to stay with everyone for ever, but Man chooses his own way of life, and this way of life frightens the energy of Love. Love cannot give inspiration to annihilation. It is unseemly for the offspring of love to live in torment when he and she are beginning to build a new life together — when they are endeavouring to establish a home in an apartment resembling a vault of lifeless stone. When each has their own work and interests and their own environment. When there is no common vision of the future, no conjugal aspirations. When their bodies are attracted by mere fleshly alleviation, only to hand over their child to the cruel ways of a world devoid of clean water, a world filled with bandits, wars and disease. It is from this that the energy of Love flees."

"But what if he and she have lots of money? Or the parents give the newlyweds, instead of a tiny flat, say a six-room apartment in a fancy modern block, with a guard on duty at the entrance, and they give them a fine car, and deposit lots of money into their bank account — would the energy of Love agree to remain under those conditions? Could he and she live their whole life in love?"

"Then they will be obliged to live their lives to the end of their years in cold fear, deprived of love and freedom. And watch everything around them grow old and rot."

"So what exactly does this finical energy of Love require?"

"Love is not finicky or obstinate, it aspires to the Divine creation. It can forever warm the heart of one who agrees to co-create with it a Space of Love."

"And is there a Space of Love somewhere in the design you have come up with?"

"Yes."

"And where is it?"

"It is in everything. First it is born for the couple, then again for their children. And through three planes of being the children will have a connection with the whole Universe.

"Imagine, Vladimir, that *he* and *she* will begin in their love to implement this design that you and I are outlining. They will plant family trees and herbs in the ground, together with an orchard. And how happy they will be in the spring when their co-creations burst forth into bloom. Love will eternally dwell between them, in their hearts, all around. And each will see the other in a spring flower, remembering how they planted a flowering tree together. And the taste of raspberries will remind them of the taste of love, since in the autumn *he* and *she* — in love for each other — touched the twig of a raspberry bush.

"In the shady orchard splendid fruit is ripening on every tree thereof. And the orchard was planted jointly by *he* and *she*. They planted the orchard in love.

"*She* laughed resoundingly when *he* dug a hole and perspiration covered his brow, and *she* wiped it off with her hand and planted a kiss on his burning lips.

"It often happens in life that only one of the partners is in love, while their mate simply tolerates the other's presence. Once they start working on the orchard, the energy of Love will multiply itself and never forsake either of them! After all, their way of life will help them both live their lives in love and convey the Space of Love to their children in continuation. And help them raise their children together with God in His image and likeness."

"Anastasia, tell me in greater detail about the raising of children. A desire to know more about this is something many readers in their letters have expressed. Even if you don't have a system of your own, at least tell us, out of the existing systems, which is best."

CHAPTER THIRTY

In His image and likeness

"You will not find a single system of child-raising that will suit everyone, Vladimir, if only because each one must first respond to the question of exactly what kind of individual they want to raise their child to be."

"What d'you mean, what kind? A Man, of course — a happy, intelligent Man."

"If so, then the parents themselves must become that kind of Man. And if they themselves have not been able to achieve happiness, then they should know what has prevented them from doing so.

"I very much want to speak about happy children. Raising them, Vladimir, means also raising yourself. The project we have been outlining all together will help in this. You and everyone else know the way children are born these days. People do not pay enough attention to their whole experience leading up to the birth, and many children are deprived of the planes of being inherent only in Man, and so children are inevitably born cripples."

"Cripples? D'you mean without arms or legs, or polio victims?"

"A Man may be born crippled not only in outward appearance. Sometimes the body may appear externally quite healthy. But Man has a second self, and each Man should have a full set of all forms of energy. Intellect, feelings, thought and much else besides. But more than half of all children, even by today's very low standards, are deemed by your medical professionals to be deficient. If you want proof of this, take a look and see how many schools there are today for the 'mentally retarded'. That's how your medical professionals classify them. Only they are comparing their abilities with those of children considered relatively normal. But if the doctors saw what the mind and the inner complexes of human energy could be in the ideal, only a few rare individuals among all the children born on the Earth would be considered 'normal'."

"But why are all children not completely perfect, as you say?"

"The technocratic world aims to prevent the three most important points in newly born children from merging into one. Technocracy tries to break Man's links with the Divine Mind. And the links are broken before the child is born. And in looking for this connection, Man goes searching the world in suffering, and does not find it."

"What 'most important points' are you talking about? What's this about 'links with the mind'? I don't get any of it."

"Vladimir, in a great many aspects Man is formed even before his entrance into the world. And his upbringing should come into contact with all creation. What God has used in creating His splendid creations should not be neglected by His son. Parents should impart to their co-creation the three most important points, the three primary planes of being.

"Here is the first point of Man's birth — it is called *parental thought*. Both the Bible and the Koran talk about it: "In the beginning was the Word"[1] — though it could be put more precisely: "In the beginning was the Thought". Let anyone calling themselves a parent today remember when they conceived their child in thought, and what kind of child they thought of him as. What kind of life did they foresee for him? What kind of world did they prepare for their creation?"

[1]John 1: 1 *(Authorised King James Bible)*.

"I think, Anastasia, that very few would even care to think of anything like that before the woman actually gets pregnant. In other words, they simply sleep together. Sometimes without even being married. And they get married when the girl gets pregnant, since there's no way of knowing whether she'll get pregnant at all. And there's no sense in thinking about it ahead of time, when there's no guarantee she'll even have a child."

"Yes, unfortunately, that is the way it often happens. Most people are conceived in fleshly indulgence. But Man, the image and likeness of God, should not come into the world as the result of fleshly indulgence.

"Now picture a different scenario. *He* and *she* build their splendid living home in love for one another and in thoughts about their future co-creation. And they visualise how their son or daughter will be happy in that place. How their offspring will hear its first sounds — its mother's breathing and the singing of the birds, God's creations. Then they will visualise how their child, when he grows up, will want to rest in his parents' garden after a hard day's journey and sit in the shade of a cedar tree. In the shade of a tree planted in love for him by his parents' hands, with thoughts of him, in their native land. The planting of the family tree on the part of the future parents will define this *first point,* and this point in turn will call upon the planets to aid them in their future co-creation. It is vital! It is important! And above all else it belongs to God! It is confirmation that you will be creating in His likeness! In the likeness of Him, the Grand Creator! And He will rejoice in the conscious awareness of His son and daughter.

"*Thought is the origin of everything.* Please believe me, Vladimir. The currents of all the diverse energies of the Universe will unite in that spot where the thoughts of two have merged into one in love, where two together are contemplating a splendid creation.

"The *second point,* or rather, yet another human plane, will be born and light a new star in the heavens when two bodies merge into one — merge in love and with thoughts of a splendid creation — in the very place where you build your Paradise home, your living home for your future child.

"Then the wife who has conceived should live in that spot for nine months. And it is best of all if these months are the blossoming of spring, the sweet fragrance of summer, and the fruits of autumn. Where nothing will distract her except for joy and pleasant feelings. Where the wife, in whom a co-creation is already dwelling splendidly, is surrounded only by the sounds of Divine creations. She lives there and feels with her whole self the whole Universe. And the future mother should see the stars. And mentally give all the stars and all the planets to her splendid child as a gift — something the mother can do all with the greatest of ease, something completely within her power. And everything will follow the mother's thought without hesitation. And the Universe will be a faithful servant to the splendid creation these two people have produced in love.

"And a *third point,* a new plane of being should come about in that space. Right there on the spot where the conception occurred the birth should take place. And the father should stay close around. And the great all-loving Father will raise over the three of them a crown."

"Wow! I don't know why, Anastasia, but I find your words even took *my* breath away. You know, I was able to visualise the spot you're talking about. And oh, how I could visualise it! It made me feel as though I wanted to be born again myself in such a place. So that right this moment I could go and rest in a splendid garden planted by my father and mother. So that I could sit in the shade of a tree planted for me before my birth. The place where I was conceived and where I was born. Where my mother walked in the garden, thinking about me, even before I came into the world."

"Such a place would greet you with great joy, Vladimir. If your body should fall ill, it would heal the body. If your soul, it would heal the soul too. And if you were weary it would give you food and drink. It would embrace you in a gentle sleep and wake you with a joyful dawn. But, as with most of the people living on the Earth today, you do not have such a spot. You do not have a native land — a Motherland — where the planes of being can merge into one."

"But why does everything we do turn out so lousy? And why do mothers continue to bring semi-retarded children into the world? Who took this spot away from me? Who has taken it away from everyone else?"

"Vladimir, perhaps you yourself can say who failed to create such a place for your daughter Polina?"

"What?! You're not suggesting I'm to blame for...? For my daughter not having a spot?"

CHAPTER THIRTY-ONE

But who is to blame?

"But I had no idea all that could be done so fine, just like that. Pity I can't turn the clock back in time and correct everything."

"But why go back? Life goes on, and each one is given the opportunity at any moment to create a splendid way of life."

"Life goes on, of course, but what good are old people, for example? Now they expect their children to help *them,* while the children themselves are unemployed. Besides, how can children be properly brought up now, when they're all grown up themselves?"

"Adults can still give their children a Divine upbringing."

"But how?"

"You know, it would be good for the elderly to apologise to their children. And sincerely apologise, for not having been able to give them a trouble-free world. For dirty water and polluted air.

"And let them begin to build, with their elderly hands, a real living home for their grown kids. If only such a splendid thought is born in them, the days of their lives will be extended. And when the elderly reach out their hand to touch their Motherland, believe me, Vladimir, the children they yearn to see will return to them. And perhaps the elderly will not be able to grow their living home completely, but their very children will be able to bury them right in their Motherland, and thereby help them come to life again."

"Bury them in their Motherland? Oh, by 'Motherland' you mean their lot of family terrain. So, we should bury our relations on this lot of land, instead of in a cemetery? And we'll put up memorials to them there?"

"Of course, on their own land, their own plot of ground. In the forest planted by their own hand. But of man-made memorials they have no need. Indeed, everything around will serve as a memorial to them. And every day everything around you will remind you of them and not with sadness, but with gladness. And your line will be immortal — after all, it is only good memories that will bring back souls to the Earth."

"Hold on, hold on there. What about the cemeteries? D'you mean to say they're completely superfluous?"

"Vladimir, cemeteries today are something like cesspits, where people throw their useless garbage. Even up until recently the bodies of those who died were buried in family tombs, chapels and temples. And only those without family or wayward people were taken outside the community. What is left today is but a distorted remembrance ritual of long ago. You go through a ritual after three days, then nine days after that, then six months, then a year, and so on. Then the remembrance is wholly superseded by the ritual itself. The souls of those who have passed away are gradually forgotten by those living today. And even the living are all too often forgotten, when children abandon their own parents and run away to some far-off land. And the children themselves are not to blame — they are simply running from what they intuitively perceive as the parents' lie and the hopelessness of their own aspirations. They are running away from impending hopelessness, only to find themselves at the same dead end.

"Everything in the Universe is arranged so that those souls who are called by good memories from the Earth are the first to be re-embodied in material form. Called not by ritual, but by genuine feelings. They will appear in those living on the Earth when the departed, by virtue of their way of life, leave behind pleasant memories of themselves. When the memories of them are not ritualistic, but are real and tangible.

"In comparison with the multitude of other human planes of being in the Universe, the human material plane is no less significant, and we must lovingly cherish our relationship to it.

"From the bodies buried in the forest they themselves planted, grass and flowers will come up, along with bushes and trees. You will see these and delight in them. Every day you will come into contact with a piece of your Motherland tilled by your parents' hand, you will communicate with them subconsciously, and they will communicate with you. Have you ever heard of guardian angels?"

"Yes, I have."

"These guardian angels, your ancestors both close and distant, will endeavour to watch over you. In three generations their souls will once again be embodied on the Earth. But even when they do not have an earthly, material incarnation, the energy of their souls will not refrain from watching over you every moment. Nobody will be able to aggressively invade your kin's terrain. The energy of fear is in each person — an energy that will also be awakened in the aggressor. The aggressor here will find himself subject to a multitude of diseases, arising from stress. In time they will also destroy him."

"'In time,' you say, but that aggressor might wreak a lot of havoc in the meantime."

"Who will seek to attack, Vladimir, if he knows that his punishment is inevitable?"

"But what if he doesn't know it?"

"Every person today knows this intuitively."

"Well, okay, let's say you're right about aggressors, but what about friends? Let's say I want to have my friends over for a visit one night. They'll come and get a fright from everything around them."

"Any friends you have whose thoughts are pure will be gladly welcomed by what is around them, as you will be glad to greet them. And here I might bring up the example of the hound. When a friend comes to the dog's owner, a faithful watchdog will not lay a paw on him. When an aggressor attacks, however, the faithful hound is ready to do mortal combat with him.

"And on your plot of Motherland even each blade of grass that grows will be healthful both to you and to your friends. And each breeze that blows will bring you healing pollen from the flowers, bushes and trees. And the energy of all your forebears will be present with you. And in anticipation of co-creation the planets themselves will await your dictation.

"And the face of your beloved will reflect from every petal of the splendid flowers in perpetuity. And the children you raise will tenderly talk with you for millennia to come. And you yourself will be embodied in new generations. And so you will talk with yourself, and help with your own upbringing. And you will produce co-creations with your Parent. In your own Motherland, in your own Space of Love will dwell the Divine energy — love!"

When Anastasia told me about the plot of land back in the taiga, my breath was simply taken away, captivated as it was by her fervour and the intonations of her voice. Later, after coming home and writing these lines, I often wondered how important it really is for each individual to have such a spot of his own — this piece of one's Motherland, as she calls it? Can one really see to a child's upbringing when he is already grown, with one's own last breath? Is it really possible, with the help of one's own family terrain, to speak with one's parents again and for their energy to protect one, both in spirit and in body? And — just imagine — it came about that all my doubts were erased all on their own by life itself. This is how it happened...

CHAPTER THIRTY-TWO

The old man at the dolmen

Three years ago I went to the northern Caucasus to write the first chapters about the dolmens, which people now flock to visit in an unending stream. But back then very few bothered to come and see these edifices of our ancient forebears. I would make frequent visits — on my own — to the dolmen situated on a property belonging to a farmer by the name of Stanislav Bambakov in the settlement of Pshada,[1] in the Gelendzhik district. And each time I went, there was old Bambakov at the dolmen. He always showed up unexpectedly, wearing a patched shirt and carrying a jar of honey from his apiary.

The elderly man was tall, lean and very agile. He had acquired his land only recently, at the beginning of *perestroika*,[2] and gave the impression he was most anxious to get everything set up on it as quickly as possible. He built himself a small house and a shed for his beehives, along with farm buildings made of various scrap materials. He started putting in an orchard and digging a small pond, thinking to coax forth a water spring, but he ran into a layer of rock.

In addition, old Bambakov was very attentive to the dolmen. He would sweep all around it. He also took the rocks he found in the field beside the dolmen and put them in a pile.

---

[1] *Pshada* — see footnote 8 in Book 2, Chapter 33: "Your sacred sites, O Russia!".

[2] *perestroika* — see footnote 3 in Chapter 19 of the present volume: "A secret science".

He told me that these rocks had been brought here manually from other places, and pointed out how different they were from other rocks in the vicinity. People had made them into a mound, he said, and erected the dolmen on top.

The old man's farmstead stood off to one side, away from the settlement and the main road. Most of the time he worked it all by himself. I wondered whether he realised how pointless his efforts were. There was no way he could set up his farmstead, work the land and build himself a regular modern house. But even if a miracle should happen and he should succeed in beautifying the surrounding land and establishing his farmstead, he would still hardly have cause for rejoicing. Everybody's children were running off to the cities. Indeed, this old man's son had set himself up with his wife in Moscow, where he'd become a civil servant.

Didn't the old man realise how pointless his efforts were? They weren't of any use to anyone, even the children. Their father would no doubt have to die with a heavy heart, knowing that his farmstead would go to ruin. Knowing that everything would grow over with wild grasses, and his bees would swarm out. And the dolmen standing so awkwardly in the middle of his field would once again get covered in garbage. He ought to have taken it easy in his advanced years, while here he was working his heart out from morning 'til night, always digging or building something like a possessed man.

One time I arrived at the dolmen well after dark. The path leading to it was lit by the light of the moon. Silence reigned — the only sound was the rustle of leaves in the breeze. I stopped a few steps short of the trees growing around the dolmen.

There sitting on a rock next to the dolmen's portico was the old man. I recognised his gaunt figure at once. Usually agile and cheerful, he sat there without so much as a stir. He appeared to be weeping. Then he got up and began pacing back and forth near the portico with his usual quick gait. Then he stopped abruptly, turned toward the dolmen and gave an affirmative wave of his hand. I realised that Bambakov was communicating with the dolmen, having a conversation with it.

I turned and headed back to the settlement, endeavouring to tread as softly as I could. Along the way I fell to wondering how this old fellow, already in his twilight years, could possibly be helped by the dolmen, no matter how strong or wise a spirit it possessed. How indeed?! Surely not just through communicating like that? *Wisdom!* Wisdom is something you need when you're young. What good is it when you're old? Who needs it? Who's going to listen to speeches of wisdom, if even one's own children are a million miles away?

Then a year and a half later, during one of my regular visits to Gelendzhik, I once again set out for the dolmen on old Bambakov's property. I already knew that Stanislav Bambakov had died. And I was a little sad that I wouldn't be seeing this cheerful, stalwart old fellow again. And I was sorry that I wouldn't have the chance to taste any more honey from his apiary. But what worried me the most was the prospect of seeing garbage around the dolmen and the whole place in a state of ruin. However...

The lane leading from the main road to the farmstead, it turned out, was freshly swept. Just before the path turned off that led to the dolmen, there among the trees stood wooden tables with benches around, even a beautiful gazebo. Along the lane, neatly marked off by whitened stones, were growing green cypress saplings. Lights burned in the windows of the little house, as well as outside, on a lamp-post.

His son! Old Bambakov's son, Sergei Stanislavovich Bambakov, had left Moscow, quit his job and moved with his wife and son here to his father's farmstead.

Sergei and I sat at one of the tables underneath the trees...

"My father rang me in Moscow, asked me to come. I came, looked around, and brought my family," recounted Sergei. "And I started working here with my dad. Such a joy it turned out to be, working alongside him. And when he died, there was no way I could leave this place."

"No regrets moving here from Moscow?"

"No regrets, and my wife has no regrets either. I thank my father every day for this. We feel a lot more at home here."

"Have you got some facilities in — running water for instance?"

"Facilities... well, you see the outhouse there — that's something my father fixed up before he died. No, I'm talking about feeling at home in a different way. You know, feeling better inside, more satisfied."

"And what about work?"

"We've got our fill of work. There's the new orchard to tend to, and looking after the apiary. I'm still not a hundred percent knowledgeable about working with bees. Too bad my father's skill didn't rub off on me.

"More and more people are coming to the dolmen, and every day we greet the touring coaches. The wife's always glad to help out. My father asked me to keep on greeting people, and I greet them. I've set up a little coach stop, I want to bring in running water. But they keep harassing us over taxes. Right now we don't really have enough to get by. At least we can be thankful that the head of the local administration can give us a little help."

I told Sergei about what Anastasia had said about land, about the lots, and remembering parents, and he responded:

"You know, she's right! She's a hundred percent right! My father died, and yet it seems as though I talk with him every day — sometimes we argue, even. And he's becoming closer and closer to me — it's as though he never died."

"What d'you mean? How can you talk with him? The way mediums do — you hear voices?"

"Of course not. It's much simpler than that. You see that crater over there? He was searching for water and stumbled across a layer of rock. I was going to fill in that crater and put another table with benches in its place. And then I thought to myself: *What have you done here, dear old dad? You didn't think things through. Now I've got extra work to do, and there's so much on my plate already.* Only the rains came, and water gushed down from the mountain and filled the crater, and it stayed — the water level stayed up for several months. A little pond formed. And I thought: *Jolly good, dad! That crater of yours is good for something after all!* And now I see there's so many other things he thought of here, I'm still trying to figure them all out."

"Can you tell me how he managed to get you to come here, Sergei, all the way from Moscow? What words did he use?"

"As far as I can recall, he used very simple words. Ordinary words. I only remember that his words gave me some kind of feelings and desires I'd never had before... and here I am. *Thank you, dad!*"

What words did old Bambakov learn when he communicated with the dolmen? What wisdom did he learn to make his son come back to him? And come back to him for good! Pity they buried him in the cemetery, and not on his own land, like Anastasia said. And I began to be even a bit envious of Sergei — his father found, or created for him, his own piece of his Motherland. Will I ever have mine? Will others have theirs? Bambakov has it good. It would be good for everyone to be able to stand on their own piece of their Motherland!

CHAPTER THIRTY-THREE

School, or the lessons of the gods

After my final visit to the dolmen on Stanislav Bambakov's property and my meeting with his son I began recalling more distinctly my conversation with Anastasia about one's Motherland, and about her 'lot' project. My head was floating in memories of the individual plots comprising splendid communities of the future which she had outlined with a stick in the moist earth. And how enthusiastically, with unusual intonations in her voice, she had endeavoured to describe them — it was as though I could hear the very leaves rustle in the gardens now covering the former wasteland, and hear the pure water gurgling in the brooks, and look and see the beautiful and happy men and women living among them. And hear the children's laughter, and the songs at the close of the day. Along with this, the extraordinary nature of her description provoked a whole range of questions, such as:

"The way you've drawn them, Anastasia, it looks as though the lots are not right up against each other. Why?"

"This splendid community has to have walkways, roadways and paths. There should be a passage no less than three metres wide on all sides between the lots."

"And will there be a school in this community?"

"Of course — look, there it is, in the middle of all the squares."

"I wonder what kind of teachers will be teaching in the new school, and how they will structure the classes. Probably the way I saw at Shchetinin's school. A lot of people are going there now. Everybody likes the forest school at Tekos.[1]

And a lot of people want to set up similar schools in their own communities."

"Shchetinin's school is indeed marvellous. It is a step toward the school where children in the new communities will study. The pupils who have gone through Shchetinin's school will help build them and teach in them. But wise and educated teachers are not the only principal component here. Parents will also be teaching their children in these new schools, and at the same time they will learn from their children."

"But how can parents become teachers all of a sudden? Will all the parents have a higher education, let alone specialised education? There are a lot of different subjects — maths, physics, chemistry, literature — who will teach the children these in the schools?"

"The level and specialisation will not be uniform, of course, for everyone on the whole. But then, after all, the study of sciences and other subjects should not be considered an end in itself, a primary goal. It is much more important to learn how to be happy, and that is something only the parents can show by their example — that is their role.

"It is not at all necessary for the parents to teach classes in the traditional sense. Parents, for example, can participate in joint discussions or collectively administer an examination."[2]

"An exam? Whose exam could the parents administer?"

"Their children's, and the children could examine them, examine their parents."

"Parents administer their kids' exams?! You're talking about school exams?! Now that has to be some kind of joke!

---

[1]*Tekos* — the name of the settlement near Gelendzhik where Mikhail Petrovich Shchetinin's school is located. For a description of the school, see Book 3, Chapter 17: "Put your vision of happiness into practice" and Chapter 18: "Academician Shchetinin".

[2]*administer an examination* — It should be remembered that in Russian schools examinations are usually oral, rather than written.

Then all the kids would end up with top marks! What parent is going to give his own child a low mark? Any parent, of course, is automatically going to mark their son or daughter near the top of the class."

"Vladimir, do not jump to conclusions. Along with classes resembling those in today's schools, the new school will have others — more important ones."

"Others? What kind of others?"

And all at once a thought crossed my mind: if Anastasia could so easily show scenes from millennial antiquity (whatever the process involved — her ray, hypnosis, or something else besides — it still worked), that means... that means, she must be able to show the near future too. So I asked her:

"Could you show me, Anastasia, at least one class from that school of the future, the kind of school that those new communities will have? Could you show me a non-traditional class?"

"I could."

"Then show me. I want to compare it with what I saw in Shchetinin's school. And with the classes I had back in my own schooldays."

"And you will not ask about or be frightened by the power that I use to create scenes of the future?"

"I don't care how you do it. It'll simply be most interesting for me to watch."

"Then lie down on the ground, relax, and doze off."

Anastasia quietly placed her hand on top of mine and...

I could see, as though from above, amidst a whole lot of plots, one which had an internal configuration different from the rest. It comprised several large wooden buildings linked by footpaths, lined on either side by a variety of flowerbeds. Near the building complex stood a natural amphitheatre: along the side of a hill rows of benches descended in a semi-circular formation. On these were seated about three hundred people of different ages, including both grey-haired elders and some quite young. It looked as though they were sitting in family groups, since adult men and women were interspersed with children of various ages. Everyone was talking excitedly amongst themselves, as though they were anticipating something out of the ordinary — a concert performance by a superstar or a presidential address.

In front of the audience on a wooden stage or platform stood two small tables and two chairs, with a large chalkboard behind. Alongside the platform there was a group of children, about fifteen in all, ranging in age from five to twelve, engaged in an animated discussion.

"This is the beginning of something resembling a symposium on astronomy," I heard Anastasia say.

"But what are the children doing here? Don't their parents have anybody they can leave them with?" I asked Anastasia.

"One of the group of children arguing amongst themselves will now give the keynote presentation," she explained. "Right now they are voting on who it shall be. There are two candidates, you see — a boy, he is nine years old, and a girl, she is eight... Now the children are voting... Ah, the majority has picked the boy."

A young boy approached one of the tables with a confident, businesslike step. From a cardboard folder he took out some papers containing designs and sketches and laid them out on the table. The rest of the group of children — some slowly and solemnly, others with a hop, skip and a jump — headed over to where their parents were seated on the benches. A little red-headed, freckle-faced girl — the other candidate, who was not chosen — walked past the table, her head held proudly in the air. The folder in her hands was a little bigger and thicker than the boy's — no doubt it too contained sketches and designs.

The boy at the table tried to say something to the girl as she went by, but she didn't stop. She simply straightened her braid and walked on past, deliberately looking the other way. For some time the boy followed her distractedly with his gaze. Then he once more focused his attention on rearranging the papers in front of him.

"Who on earth could have managed to teach these kids enough astronomy so that they can make a presentation before a group of adults?" I asked Anastasia.

And she replied:

"Nobody taught them. They were given the opportunity to work out for themselves how the whole Universe is structured, to prepare their arguments and present their conclusions. They have been working on it for more than two weeks already, and the final moment has come. They will now defend their views, and their conclusions may be refuted by anyone who wishes to do so."

"So, it turns out this is some kind of game?"

"You can think of what is going on here as a 'game'. Only it is very serious. Each person present will now have their thinking about the planetary order accelerated, and may perhaps start contemplating something even greater than that. After all, the children have been thinking and pondering for two weeks now, and their thought is not limited by anything — there are no dogmas or theories of planetary order to weigh them down. We still do not know what they will come up with."

"They'll be fantasising with their child mindsets, you mean to say?"

"I mean to say, they shall present their own theories. After all, even adults have not come up with any proven truths regarding planetary order. The goal of this symposium is not to work out any canons, but to accelerate thought, which afterward will determine what is true, or at least come closer to the truth."

At this point a young man stepped up to the second table and announced the presentation was about to begin. Whereupon the nine-year-old started to speak.

He spoke confidently and enthusiastically for about twenty-five or thirty minutes. What he said struck me as sheer childish fantasy — a fantasy not grounded in any scientific theories or even an elementary knowledge one would get from a high-school astronomy course. He spoke in substance as follows:

"If you look up to the sky in the late evening, you see a whole lot of stars shining there. There are different kinds of stars. Some stars are little and others a little larger. But very small stars can be big, too. Only we think at first that they are little. But they are very big. Because when an aeroplane flies very high, it is small, but when it is on the ground and we walk up to it, it turns out to be big, and it can hold a whole lot of people. And each star could hold a whole lot of people.

"Only there are no people on the stars right now. But they shine in the evening. The big ones shine, and the little ones too. They shine so we can see them and think about them. The stars want us to make the things we do on the Earth just as good on them too. They are a little envious of the Earth. They really want berries and trees to grow on them the way they do here, they want the same little streams and fishes.

"The stars are waiting for us, and each of them is trying to shine to make us pay attention to it. But we can't yet travel to them, 'cause we've got a lot of things to take care of here at home. But when we do take care of everything at home, and things are good everywhere on the whole Earth, then we shall travel to the stars. Only we shan't travel by plane or rocket ship, 'cause flying by plane would take too long and the rocket ship would be long and boring. Besides, we won't all fit into a plane or a rocket ship. And there won't be room for all sorts of things we want to take with us. There won't be any room for trees, or a stream. But once we make everything right all over the Earth, we'll fly the whole Earth to the nearest star.

"Besides, some stars will want to come to Earth themselves and snuggle up to it. They have already sent their fragments, and their fragments have snuggled up to the Earth. People used to think that these were comets, but they are fragments of stars which really, really wanted to snuggle up to our beautiful Earth. They were sent by the stars, which are waiting for us. We can fly the whole Earth to a far-off star, and whoever wants to can remain on the star, to make it beautiful, like on the Earth."

All this time the boy had been holding up his sheets of paper and showing them to the audience. They contained drawings of a starry sky and the Earth's trajectory as it headed toward the stars. The last drawing portrayed two stars blossoming with gardens and the Earth moving away from them on its intergalactic journey.

When the boy finished talking and showing the drawings, the master of ceremonies announced that anyone who wished could challenge him or put forth his own views on what had just been said. But no one hastened to speak. Everybody remained silent — it looked to me as though they were concerned about something.

"What are they hesitating for?" I asked Anastasia. "Don't any of the adults here know about astronomy?"

"They are hesitating because they know whatever arguments they put forth must be clear and well thought through. After all, their children are present. If what they say is not understandable or acceptable to the children's hearts, then the speaker will risk being mistrusted or, even worse, treated unsympathetically. Adults cherish their relationship with their children, and hesitate to risk any harm to it. They are afraid of incurring the audience's disfavour — especially their children's."

The heads of many in the audience began turning in the direction of a grey-haired elderly man sitting in their midst.

He had his arm around the shoulders of the little red-haired girl sitting beside him, the same one who had been one of the candidates to give the keynote presentation. Sitting next to them was a young and very beautiful woman. Anastasia commented:

"A lot of people now have their eyes on the elderly man in the middle of the audience. He is a university professor, a scientist, now retired. His personal life got mixed up rather early on, and he had no children. Ten years ago he procured a lot of land, and began to establish a home on it all by himself. A young woman fell in love with him and the little red-headed girl was born to them. The young woman next to him is his wife and the mother of his child. The retired professor very much loves the child of his old age. And the girl, his daughter, treats him with great respect and love. Many of those present here today believe that the professor is entitled to take the floor first."

But the elderly professor had trouble getting his first words out. I could see him nervously rumpling the pages of some journal with his hands. Finally he got up and started to speak. He said something about the structure of the Universe, the comets and the mass of the Earth, and finally summed up his remarks something like this:

"The planet Earth, of course, is moving through space and rotating. But it is inextricably linked with the solar system, and cannot move independently. It cannot leave the solar system and travel to distant galaxies. The Sun gives life to everything living on the Earth. Moving away from the Sun would involve a serious cooling of the Earth, and we would end up with a dead planet. We can all observe what happens even when we move just a fraction away from the Sun. We get winter."

At this point the professor stopped abruptly. The boy who had presented the paper flipped distractedly through his sketches, then gave a questioning glance to his peers in the group, the ones who had helped him prepare the presentation. But it was apparent that everybody had found the argument of winter and cooling very cogent and plausible. This argument had the effect of crushing the children's beautiful dream of a space-travelling Earth. And all at once in the ensuing quiet, which had lasted a half-minute already, the voice of the elderly professor once more sounded forth.

"Winter... Life can't help but slow down if the Earth doesn't get enough solar energy. Simply can't help! You don't need any scientific studies to see that, to be convinced... On the other hand... it *is* possible that the Earth itself possesses energy, the same as the Sun. Only it hasn't yet manifested itself. Nobody's discovered it yet. Perhaps you yourselves will discover it at some point. Perhaps it is possible that the Earth could be self-sufficient. This energy will be made manifest in some way... The Sun's energy will show itself on the Earth, and, like solar energy, it will be able to unfold the petals of the flowers. And then we can travel on the Earth across the galaxy... Yes, then..."

The professor lost his train of thought and fell silent. A murmur of dissatisfaction could be heard through the audience. And then it all began...

The adults in the audience began getting up from their seats and holding forth, denouncing the professor, especially the possibility of living without the Sun. Some of them spoke of the photosynthesis of plants, others about environmental temperature, still others about the fixed nature of planetary trajectories. Through all this the professor sat with an increasingly drooping head. His red-haired daughter turned her head to look at each of the speakers — on occasion she would try standing up, as though she were trying to protect her father from his challengers.

An elderly woman who looked like the teacher type took the floor and started holding forth on how it wasn't right to

appease or flatter children just to curry a favourable attitude
toward you on their part.

"Any lie will be exposed with time, and then how will we
all look then? This isn't just a lie, it's cowardice!" said the
woman.

The red-headed girl tugged on the lapels of her father's
jacket. She began shaking him, practically crying, her voice
breaking as she kept at him:

"Papochka,[3] you lied about the energy... Did you lie, Papochka? Because we're children? The lady called you a coward. Is that bad?"

A silence fell upon the large open-air amphitheatre. The
professor raised his head, looked his daughter in the eye, put
his hand on her shoulder and quietly said:

"I believed what I said, daughter."

At first the girl remained silent. Then she quickly stood up
on the bench and cried out as loudly as her little child's voice
could muster:

"My Papa's not a coward. Papa believed what he said. *He believed it!*"

The little girl surveyed the now hushed audience. Nobody
was even glancing in their direction. She looked at her mother. But the young woman turned away with her head lowered;
she fiddled with the buttons on the sleeve of her cardigan,
undoing them and doing them up again. The girl once more
surveyed the hushed audience, and looked at her father. As
before, the professor seemed to be gazing helplessly at his little daughter. Once more, this time in the absolute quiet, the
red-headed girl's voice sounded gently and tenderly.

"People don't believe you, Papochka. They don't believe
you 'cause the Sun's energy has not yet showed itself on the
Earth — the energy that is like the Sun and can open the petals

[3]*Papochka* (pronounced *PAH-poch-ka*) — an endearing form of *Papa*.

of the flowers. But once it appears, then everybody will believe you. They will believe you later, when it appears. Later..."

And all at once the professor's daughter quickly straightened her hair, then leapt out into the aisle and ran off. She ran to the edge of the amphitheatre, and hurried toward one of the nearby houses. She disappeared inside, only to reappear in the doorway a few seconds later. This time the girl was holding in her hands an earthenware pot with a plant in it. She ran with it over to the speaker's table, which was now vacant. She put the potted plant down on the table. And her child's voice, now loud and confident, resonated over the heads of the audience:

"Look, here's a flower. Its petals are closed. All the flowers' petals have closed. 'Cause there's no sun out today. But they will open, because there is energy on the Earth... I shall... I shall transform myself into the energy which can open the petals of flowers."

With that the little girl closed her hands into a fist and began staring at the flower. She went on staring without blinking.

The people sitting in their seats refrained from conversation. Everyone was looking at the little girl and the plant in the earthenware pot on the table in front of her.

Slowly the professor rose from his seat and went over to his daughter. He went up to her and put his hands on her shoulders, trying to lead her away. But the little redhead shrugged him off and whispered:

"Why don't you help me instead, Papochka!"

The professor was no doubt utterly bewildered. He remained standing at his daughter's side, his hands on her little shoulders, and he too began staring at the flower.

But nothing was happening with the flower. And I began to feel somehow sorry for the little girl and her professor-father. But he really got himself into a fix with his declaration of faith in some kind of undiscovered energy!

All at once a boy stood up in the front row — the same boy that had given the presentation. He partially turned toward the silent audience, sniffed his nose and headed over to the table on the stage. Solemnly and confidently he approached the table and stood next to the red-haired girl. Just like her, he fixed his gaze firmly on the plant in the earthenware pot. But as far as the plant was concerned, of course, nothing was happening.

And then I saw it! I saw how children of all ages began rising from their seats and one by one came down to the stage. They silently took up a position, staring intently at the flower. The last little girl, about six years old, was carrying her very small brother in her arms. She managed to squeeze in front of those standing and someone helped her stand her younger brother up on the chair by the table. The toddler, after taking a good look at everyone around, turned to the flower and began blowing on it.

And all at once the potted plant began to gradually unfold the petals of one of its flowers. Little by little. But it didn't escape the notice of the hushed crowd in the amphitheatre. And several of them rose silently from their seats. And now, on the table, a second flower was already opening its petals, along with a third, and a fourth...

"Oooh..." cried the teacher-type in an excited, childlike voice, and began clapping her hands. Then the whole amphitheatre broke into applause. The beautiful young woman ran over to her professor-husband, who by this time had stepped off to one side of the crowd of delighted children surrounding the flower and was rubbing his forehead. She leapt at him on the run, threw her arms around his neck and began kissing his cheeks and lips...

The little redhead took a step in the direction of her embracing parents, but the boy who had given the presentation stopped her. She managed to wriggle her hand away, but after taking a few more steps, she turned, went up close to him and buttoned up a button which had become undone on his shirt. With that she gave him a smile, then quickly turned and ran off to her still embracing parents.

More and more people were now heading from their seats down to the stage, some with babes in arms, others shaking the hand of the young presenter. He just stood there, his arm outstretched for handshaking, while his second hand was clasping the button the little girl had just done up for him.

All at once someone struck up a tune on a bayan[4] — something between a gypsy melody and a Russian folk dance. And when some old fellow began stamping his feet on the stage, he was joined by a plumpish lady who made her entrance like a swan. And two young fellows had already launched into a boisterous *prisiadka*.[5] And the flower with its unfolding petals watched as more and more people got carried away by the tricky and boisterous rhythms of a Russian folk dance.

Then, all of a sudden, the scene of the unusual school disappeared, as though a screen had been turned off. I was sitting on the ground. Taiga vegetation stretched all around, as far as the eye could see, and there beside me was Anastasia.

[4]*bayan* — in this case a Russian folk-instrument of the accordion family, using a single reed and a chromatic scale, with rows of buttons on both the left and the right sides (not to be confused with a similarly named bass drum in India). Derived from another accordion-type instrument, the diatonic *garmon'*, it is often played together with a stringed instrument (such as the *domra* or *balalaika*). It takes its name from a legendary Russian singer-storyteller named Bayan or Boyan, whose songs inspired ancient warriors to do their utmost in battle. By extension, the word *bayan* (derived from an ancient Russian verb signifying 'to tell') could refer to any wandering poet-storyteller — a counterpart of the Celtic *bard*.

[5]*prisiadka* (pronounced *prees-YAT-ka*) — one of the more famous Slavic dances, usually performed by men, involving squatting on one knee while kicking out the opposite leg in front, then alternating the leg positions in quick succession.

Inside me, however, a kind of excitement lingered, and I could still hear the laughter of happy people and the sounds of the cheery dance music, which I didn't want to let go of. When the sounds within me gradually died down, I said to Anastasia:

"What you showed me just now is nothing at all like any school class I've ever seen. It's some kind of family gathering, of families living in the community. And there wasn't a single teacher there — everything happened all by itself."

"There was a teacher, Vladimir, a very wise teacher. But he purposely did not attract anyone's attention to himself."

"But why were the parents there? Their emotional reactions only provoked stress."

"Emotions and feelings can accelerate thought by a factor of many times. They have lessons like that every week in this school. Teachers and parents are united in their aspirations, and children consider themselves to be equal with adults."

"All the same, it seems weird to think of parents participating in their children's education. After all, parents aren't trained to be teachers."

"It is sad, Vladimir, that people have got into the habit of handing over their children to others to be raised, regardless of who these others are — a school, or some other institution. They simply hand their children over, often not knowing what kind of world-view will be inculcated in them, or what destiny awaits them as a result of somebody's particular teaching. By giving their children over to an uncertain future, they are actually depriving themselves of their own children. That is why children whom mothers hand over to someone else to be taught learning often forget their mothers in turn."

The time came to leave. My mind was filled up full with all the information I had acquired, so much so that I was scarcely aware of my surroundings. I took my leave of Anastasia in some haste. I told her:

"Don't bother seeing me off. When I'm walking alone, I can think unhindered."

"Yes, do not let anyone hinder your thinking," she responded. "When you come to the river, my grandfather will be there, and he will help ferry you across to the landing."

I walked alone through the taiga in the direction of the river and thought about everything I had seen and heard, all at the same time. But one question persisted above all others: how did we get into this situation ('we' meaning the majority of people)? We think everyone has their Motherland, and yet none of us has a little piece of Motherland to call their own. And there isn't even any law in our country, no law guaranteeing a Man or his family the opportunity to own in perpetuity a single hectare of land. Political leaders and parties in their ever-changing procession promise all sorts of benefits, but they all manage to avoid the question concerning a piece of our Motherland. Why?

And yet our grand Motherland consists precisely of little pieces. Native, small family homesteads, with little houses and gardens on them. If nobody has anything like that, then what does our Motherland consist of? A law must be drawn up to guarantee everyone their piece of Motherland. For every family that wants one. The deputies[6] can pass such a law. The deputies are chosen by all of us. That means we must vote people into office who agree to pass such a law.

A law! How should it be worded? Maybe this way?

---

[6] *deputies* — members of the Russian *Duma,* or national parliament.

The State is obliged to provide each family couple, upon request, one hectare of land for use in perpetuity, with right of inheritance. Agricultural yields on these family lands shall never be subject to any kind of taxation. Family lands are not subject to sale.

Something like that would be okay. But what if somebody takes the land and doesn't do anything with it? Then the law should also state:

If over a period of three years the land is not cultivated, the State may take it back.

But what if some people want to live and work in the city and use their family domain like a dacha? Well, let them. Women will still come to their kin's domain[7] to give birth. Those who do not will not be forgiven later by their children.

And just who will push this law through to final adoption? A political party? Which one? We need to set up a party for this purpose.[8] And just who will take care of organising it? Where do we find politicians like that? We must seek them

---

[7]The terms *family domain* and *kin's domain* are used here interchangeably to translate the Russian term *rodovoe pomestie*. *Pomestie* is equivalent to *domain*, *estate* or *homestead*. *Rodovoe* comes from the same root as *Rod* (signifying 'God the Creator', 'origin', 'birth' or 'kin') and *Rodina* ('Motherland'); it literally means 'belonging to one's kin' and points to the unity of the past, present and future generations of one's family. Both *kin* and *family*, as used henceforth in the Ringing Cedars Series, include the whole range of one's ancestors and descendants and not merely the present generation of a family. Interestingly enough, the concept of *kin's domain* is not unlike the concept underlying the English word *kingdom*, since *king* originally meant 'head of a kin or family clan', while *dom* stems from a root signifying 'home place' or 'domain'. For more on *Rodina* see footnote 1 in Chapter 24 above: "Take back your Motherland, people!".

[8]*a party* — see footnote 3 in Chapter 26: "Even today everyone can build a home".

out, somehow. As soon as possible! Otherwise you could die, and not once come nigh to your Motherland. And your grand-children won't remember you. When will an opportunity like this come again? When will it be possible to say, "Greetings, my Motherland!"?

Anastasia's grandfather was sitting on a log by the shore. Nearby a small wooden boat was tied up, rocking ever so gen-tly on the waves. I knew it wasn't too hard to row to the near-est landing a few kilometres downstream on the other side of the river,[9] but how would he fare coming back against the current, I wondered as I greeted the old fellow. I asked him about it.

"I'll make it by and by," answered Anastasia's grandfather. Always cheery as a rule, on this occasion he seemed rather sombre and not much inclined to conversation.

I sat down beside him on the log.

"I can't understand," I said, "how Anastasia can hold so much information inside her — how she can recall things from the past and know everything that is going on in our lives right now. And here she lives way out in the taiga, and delights in the flowers, the Sun and all the little creatures. It's as though she doesn't think about anything."

"What's there to think about?" her grandfather replied. "She feels it, this information. When she needs it, she takes as much as she wants. The answers to all questions are right

---

[9]*the river* — the Ob, which flows from south to north.

here in space, right with us. We need only know how to perceive them and make them manifest."

"How do we do that?"

"How... How... Say you're walking along the street of a city you know very well, thinking about your own affairs, and a passer-by suddenly comes up to you and asks how to get somewhere. Can you give him an answer?"

"Sure."

"You see how simple it all is. You were thinking about something completely different. The question put to you has absolutely no connection with what you were thinking about, and yet you are still able to give an answer. The answer 'lives' in you."

"But that's just a request for directions. But if the same passer-by were to ask me what happened in the city we're in — let's say, a thousand years before we met, no Man could give an answer to that."

"He couldn't if he's lazy or neglectful. Everything, right from the very moment of creation, is stored in and around each individual Man... Why don't you get into the boat? Time to push off."

The old fellow took the oars. When we had got about a kilometre from our departure point on the shore, Anastasia's erstwhile taciturn grandfather began to talk.

"Try not to wallow in all your information and contemplations, Vladimir. Decide what's real by yourself. With your self, you should be able to feel both matter and what you cannot see in equal measure."

"Why are you telling me this? I don't understand."

"Because you've started digging around in all that information, trying to define it with your mind. But you won't get it with your mind. The mind can't possibly fathom the volume of information known to my granddaughter. And you'll stop being aware of the creative process taking place around you."

"I'm aware of everything — the river, the boat..."

"If you're aware of everything, then why weren't you able to say a proper good-bye to my granddaughter and your son?"

"Well, maybe I wasn't able to after all. You see, I was thinking more globally."

I had indeed left almost without saying good-bye to Anastasia, and I got so immersed in thought during my whole journey back to the river that I hardly noticed the time, but suddenly found myself on the riverbank. I added:

"Anastasia also thinks about other things, she thinks globally, she doesn't need a whole lot of sentimental gestures."

"Anastasia feels with her self all planes of being. She doesn't feel one at the expense of another."

"So?"

"Take your field-glasses out of your bag and have a look back at the tree on the bank where we pushed off."

I got out my field-glasses and had a look. Standing there by the tree-trunk, holding our son in her arms, was Anastasia. On her bent arm hung a little bundle. She stood there with our son and waved her hand at our boat, which was moving further and further away downstream. And I waved back.

"Looks as though my granddaughter and her son followed you. She was waiting for you to finish your contemplating and start thinking of your son, and of her too. And she gathered together that bundle for you. But it seemed the information you had gathered from her was more important to you.

"The spiritual and the material — you need to feel it all in equal measure. Then you'll be able to take a solid stand in life, with both feet planted firmly on the ground. When one predominates over the other, it's like a person going lame."

The old man spoke with no trace of anger as he handled the oars with dexterity.

I tried to respond aloud, either to him or to myself:

"Most of all now I need to understand... To understand things for myself! Who are we? Where are we?"

CHAPTER THIRTY-FOUR

Anomalies at Gelendzhik

Dear readers, everything I have written in these books I either heard from Anastasia, or saw and experienced myself. All the events I describe are real events from my own life, and my descriptions, especially in the first couple of books, included people's real names and addresses — a decision I later had cause to regret. These people came to be bothered more and more by curious busybodies.

Another thorny problem has been all the various rumours, events and phenomena attached to both myself and Anastasia. The particular interpretations of these events — and, consequently, the particular conclusions drawn therefrom — have also been upsetting. Many of them I cannot agree with at all. For example, I am dead set against worshipping the dolmens. I believe that we can and must communicate with the dolmens on the basis of respect, but not worship them.

The readers of the Anastasia books comprise people of various faith groups and religious confessions, with various levels of education. I believe that anyone's interpretation of events is worth our attention. Everyone has the right to their own opinion, but when expressing it, they should say: "This is my opinion, my suggestion." And of course one should not mystify everything right off, and should certainly not mystify either me or Anastasia. Otherwise one may transform Anastasia from a Man — albeit not a very ordinary Man — into some kind of extraordinary being. Might it not be that she in fact is a *supremely normal* Man, and we are the ones who are abnormal? So please excuse me for getting carried away here

with my own opinions. It's on account of my being disturbed
by a particular set of circumstances:

Rumours are circulating lightning fast at the moment
about the fiery sphere with which Anastasia communicates.
I ask my readers to recall my various descriptions of it in previous books — how this sphere appeared next to Anastasia
in emergency situations: how it first appeared when little
Anastasia was crying over her parents' grave, and then taught
her to take her first little baby steps, and how it defended her
when she was attacked. To her grandfather's question, "What
is it?" she replied: "I would call it *Good*."[1]

Yes, she does communicate with it, but even she does not
fully comprehend what kind of natural phenomenon it is.

Now why have I all of a sudden brought up the fiery sphere
which appeared out of nowhere? Because according to a mass
of witnesses, it was this very sphere that appeared in the sky
over Gelendzhik and stirred up a good deal of turmoil. Now
rumours are being spread by detractors to the effect that
Anastasia can practically bomb anyone she doesn't like with
the help of this sphere, and that she communicates not only
with the forces of light but also with the dark forces. And
here the readers themselves are adding fat to the fire. I have
already had a request from Tuapse to send this sphere to the
Sochi city hall so that they might see the light the way the
Gelendzhik council did.[2]

I shall now attempt, dear readers, to offer you a true account of what really happened in Gelendzhik, and I would
ask you to read it calmly and understandingly.

A local non-profit organisation in Gelendzhik was preparing to hold a readers' conference on the *Anastasia* books. The

[1]See Book 2, Chapter 27: "The anomaly"; also Book 3, Chapter 7: "Assault!".
[2]*Gelendzhik, Tuapse, Sochi* — cities on the eastern shore of the Black Sea (see
footnote 2 in Book 1, Chapter 30: "Author's message to readers").

relationship of the organisation's board with the city council was, to put it mildly, tense. And in Book 2 I had already given a rather unflattering portrayal of the old city leadership. Against a background like that, you can just imagine what happened.

Some time after noon on 17 September 1999, on the eve of the reader's conference, a wind blew up in the city, and a thunderstorm began. All at once a fiery sphere appeared on the small square in front of the city hall. Its subsequent behaviour, people now say, was very much like that of Anastasia's sphere.

The sphere which appeared over Gelendzhik somehow evaded the lightning-rods of the surrounding buildings, and made contact with a tree standing in the middle of the square. Then the sphere emitted several fiery spheres or rays of somewhat smaller proportions. One of them flew into the Mayor's office, flew around the room right in front of onlookers and then flew out.

A second sphere flew into the window of the Deputy Mayor, Galina Nikolaevna,[3] and hovered in the air for a while. Then it went over to the window and etched on the windowpane a strange symbol that nobody has yet been able to erase, and then flew off.

Subsequent rumours have it that the Gelendzhik administrative council has become 'holy' or 'enlightened'. They say that right after the incident with the fiery sphere, the council decided to adopt measures for a more favourable reception of the readers of my books coming to the city from out of town, to fix up the dolmens in the area, hold an annual inspirational

---

[3]*Galina Nikolaevna* — Note: *Nikolaevna* is a patronymic (i.e., a middle name derived from one's father's first name), not a surname. The combination of first name and patronymic is a common polite form of address in Russian, especially in business relationships.

songwriters' festival, and a lot more besides, which it was unwilling to do before.

Rumours of what had happened spread, together with the
affirmation that Anastasia's sphere had visited Gelendzhik.
I tried countering that it was only ball lightning, and that
its resemblance in behaviour to what I had described in the
book was purely coincidental, and the city council would
have adopted some kind of resolution, regardless. But they
would have none of it. They immediately began arguing that
there are no coincidences, and besides, it wasn't just one co-
incidence in this case, but a whole chain. And they further
declared that when coincidences follow one after another in a
chain, it can be termed a pattern.

Of course one could say that the coincidences *had* come
together in a chain. For now, at least, there was no logical explanation for the sphere bypassing the lightning-rods. Why
did it make contact with the big tree standing in the square,
flare up and make thundering sounds over it, yet refrain from
destroying it and fly over to the city council windows? Why
did it fly right into the offices of the very people capable of
taking decisions with respect to readers coming to the city?
Why did the city council render a favourable decision on a
whole lot of questions immediately afterward? Why did the
chairman of the municipal assembly take it upon herself to
personally welcome the conference delegates the next day?
And so forth.

According to one recent rumour the Mayor of Gelendzhik
and the whole administrative apparatus has changed so
much that now Gelendzhik will start to flourish, and become, as Anastasia said, "richer than Jerusalem or Rome".[4]
Another rumour has it that the sphere simply struck fear in
everyone.

---

[4]See Book 2, last page of Chapter 32: "Title!".

Upon my arrival at Gelendzhik I met with the Mayor and her deputy. I saw the symbol the sphere had etched on the glass and I touched it. I sensed an unusual aroma in the office, something similar to incense or sulphur. But there was no sensation of fright. On the contrary: Galina Nikolaevna, the Deputy Mayor, for example, even seemed more cheery than on previous occasions. She also recounted to me how everything had happened, and asked me whether I thought this might be some kind of sign.

Altogether, the way things turned out, the theory about ordinary ball lightning was quite unacceptable. And I got accused of simplifying the situation.

I don't deny that I really did try to simplify things — and not only this situation. Why? Because I have heard reports about how certain religious leaders are frightening people with their speculations on Anastasia's unusual powers — saying that these powers were not of God, and that Anastasia was not a Man. They're writing articles about this in their religious journals. I can only imagine the exaggerations that will now come up with the appearance of the sphere at Gelendzhik.

I am not about to try to either prove or refute the identification of the fiery sphere at Gelendzhik with Anastasia's — there's no sense in it now. Everybody's going to stick to their own opinion. All I want is to try to reason a little together with you, dear readers, as to what kind of forces the fiery sphere at Gelendzhik might have represented.

The Bible says: "By their fruits ye shall know them."[5] Well then, what are the fruits?

First, the fiery sphere caused no damage to the city hall. Even the glass on which it etched its symbol wasn't broken. The lingering aroma in the office was not an unpleasant one. Galina Nikolaevna (the occupant of the office) spoke with me

---

[5]Matth. 7: 20.

in the presence of four people, and none of them detected any sense of fear in her.

The sphere made thundering noises over the tree in the square, and there was a bright flare — people said it looked as though the tree itself was flaring up. But there it is, still growing away in perfect health.

The city council resolved to improve the level of service to readers from out-of-town. It also made a decision to offer regular, properly organised excursions to the dolmens Anastasia spoke about.

I myself cannot see a single negative consequence. Therefore, the fruits must be judged positive.

Anastasia says about the fiery sphere that it acts completely self-sufficiently, that it cannot be ordered about — one can only make a request of it.

In my books I am attempting to describe, as accurately as I can, situations I have seen with my own eyes, experienced with my own feelings or heard with my own ears. As for the incident with the fiery sphere at Gelendzhik, well, everyone can put forth their own version of events. But I certainly don't want anyone using this incident for the purpose of frightening people.

Besides, if one were to continue along that line, then it is possible to mystify the most mundane situations. Now people are even starting to say that this fiery sphere assisted me in making my presentation at Gelendzhik. But that's not true. I don't have any connection with it at all. And the press has not been blameless in feeding these rumours.

The respected magazine *Ogonyok*[6] printed a long article in which the author states that "an experiment is being

---

[6]*Ogonyok* (stress on last syllable) — one of the oldest weekly illustrated magazines in Russia (published since 1899). The name literally means 'little flame'.

conducted on this country on a major scale". Specifically he notes about me that "he talked on stage for eight hours straight — I haven't seen oratory like that for a long time". And another paper adds: "through all this he remained fresh as a cucumber". All these descriptions, to put it mildly, are exaggerated and inaccurate.

In the first place, at the conference I spoke not for eight hours straight, but only six. Two hours were 'added' from my presentation on the following day.

As far as assistance goes, it really was there, but with no mysticism.

On the eve of the Gelendzhik conference Anastasia came to see me, telling me I should get a good night's sleep. She offered me a tea extract that she had brought with her from the taiga, for me to drink just before bedtime. I agreed, since lately I really hadn't been able to sleep much at night. Then, when I lay down, she sat down beside me, took my hand — as she used to do back in the taiga (I described this in my chapter "Touching Paradise"[7]). And I fell asleep, as though literally flying off somewhere. Whenever she did this in the taiga, a sense of peace would always come over me.

I awoke the next morning to see a beautiful day out, I felt in top shape, and my mood was cheerful.

For breakfast Anastasia offered me only cedar milk, saying it was better not to eat any meat, since a lot of energy would be spent on digesting it. And after the cedar milk I didn't even feel like having meat. Whenever I have cedar milk, I never feel like having anything else.

When I gave my talk to the readers at the conference, Anastasia was not beside me. She stood quietly for a while in the auditorium among the readers, then went off and disappeared altogether.

[7]*"Touching Paradise"* — Chapter 21 in Book 1.

But after the publication of the articles and the rumours giving a mystic interpretation to my presentation at the conference, I began to wonder myself whether Anastasia had somehow been helping me, and I said to her:

"Don't tell me, Anastasia, you quite forgot I was supposed to look tired, at least toward the end of my presentation? Why did you let these people indulge in mystical speculation?"

She laughed, and replied:

"What kind of mysticism can there be in someone well-rested talking in a good mood with his friends? As for your speaking for so long, this was because your thought is still confused, you tried to grasp hold of a number of topics at once. It was possible to have phrased it more clearly and concisely, but you were not able to do that — also on account of the fact that your shoes were too tight and squeezing your feet, so that the blood had trouble circulating through your veins."

You see now how utterly simple in fact it all was. There was absolutely no mysticism in my presentation.

Dear readers! I'm receiving more and more letters from you asking why neither I nor the Anastasia Foundation are responding to the critical articles in the press, to the insults and accusations of bigotry directed at me and my readers in general. What a waste of time that would be! Anyway, what's the sense of responding to people who are simply out to provoke a scandal?

In November one journalist (by the name of By... — I'm not going to spell it out in full, no need to immortalise him) saw fit to publish one and the same article under different titles in no less than five publications at the same time. He changed the titles, transposed a few sentences in the text and signed himself with different names. He naturally disparages me and then rants away with a diatribe on morals, ethics and commercialism. His editors will deal with him themselves before too long. I know how distasteful such a situation can be for editors. And it's considered highly unethical in journalists' circles. After all, each publication paid him an honorarium on the understanding they were getting an 'exclusive'. What's the point of my arguing with him? Maybe the poor fellow needs the money to buy himself a decent meal. And as for the muck and lies he dishes out, I don't think they'll ever stick to Anastasia — they'll all fall back on him.

Let's face it: Anastasia's a pretty hot topic right now, so I wouldn't be surprised if a few more publications tried to capitalise on her popularity. After all, you readers number more than a million already. Let's say I start a polemic with a tabloid of maybe 50,000 subscribers. You are naturally going to want to read it, and that means you'll be giving a huge boost to their circulation. There's absolutely no sense in arguing with them. You know yourselves, after all, whether you're bigots or not. *If you really want to get back at a publication, your best bet is simply to refuse to buy it, or cancel your subscription if you have one.*

As for me, the only way I can communicate with you is through my books. So now I'm going to try and answer some of your questions.

First of all, at the present time I'm not engaged in any business activities — I spend my whole time writing. I don't belong to any religious group. I'm simply trying to come up with my own sense of what life's all about. But the criticisms and fabrications directed at me and Anastasia are likely to increase. Seems a lot of people see Anastasia as an obstacle to their own pet plans.

You can bet they'll expose themselves sooner or later. But one thing that seems pretty clear to me now is that this Siberian girl's being seen as one hell of a threat to more than a few religious groups and at the same time to some financial-industrial empires both here in Russia and abroad.

They're the ones that are persistently blowing up the question in the press: *Does Anastasia exist or not? And just who is Megré?* And then they give their own answer: *No, she doesn't. And Megré's a penny-pinching entrepreneur.* In actual fact, they are more aware than just about anyone else of Anastasia's existence.

But they feel a need to go to any length to distract people from the central message of what information is coming out, to cut off the source of information at any cost, try to take control of it, and if that doesn't work, to exterminate it.

It seems they have been better and quicker than we have at evaluating the information coming from Anastasia. They even laugh at those who question Anastasia's existence. Think about it: would anyone listening to information on the radio question the existence of the station broadcasting it? But while some self-professed 'wise guys' have got caught up in an endless round of asking *Does she exist or not?,* in the meantime there has been an intense buying up and exporting of cedar nuts in the Irkutsk, Tomsk and Novosibirsk regions — for foreign currency, yet. According to reports out of Novosibirsk and Tomsk, Chinese representatives have been involved.[8]

1999 was a banner year for cedar nut crops in many parts of Siberia. But the Novosibirsk medical factory[9] is not

---

[8]Indeed, China's domestic *consumption* of pine nuts ('cedar nuts' in Russia) is estimated to be greater than its total domestic *production.* Yet, China is the largest exporter of pine nuts to America (controlling over 90% of US imports, worth tens of millions of dollars each year). The 'Chinese' pine nuts found in North American health food stores and supermarkets are predominantly Russian in origin — they are, in fact, the nuts of Siberian cedar and Korean cedar trees 'exported' across the border to China, to be shelled and sent overseas, often without the necessary level of refrigeration.

increasing its output of cedar oil. There is a shortage of cedar nuts — the same nuts which are being made into expensive medicines in the West, where the manufacturers are taking great pains to conceal the identity of the main ingredient. Remember I wrote back in Book 1 about how they were shipping cedar nuts abroad? And when I tried searching for information about cedar nut oil, I got a warning from Poland to back off.[10] This year they've managed again to hold their own. But as to the future, well, we shall see. In the next book I shall tell about a certain surprise being prepared by Anastasia.

I am an entrepreneur. My idea was to write the books I promised and then get back to business. And I never hid my intentions from anyone — in fact I wrote about them right in Book 2.[11] But now my plans have changed. Let other Siberian entrepreneurs compete for trade with these Western smart alecs.

My plans changed because those behind critical publications continue to insult and frighten readers, labelling as bigots anybody who bothers to read my books, which they consider silly and devoid of literary value. Granted, I don't have any higher education, or experience in the literary field, and those who have these are irritated by the popularity of my books. They are especially upset by the fact that, given my level of education, I still refuse to submit my work to editors.

And they are simply furious over my publication of the five-hundred-page collection of readers' letters and poems entitled *The soul of Russia sings in Anastasia's ray*.[12] Again, I didn't

---

[9]*Novosibirsk medical factory* — see Ch. 24: "Take back your Motherland, people!".

[10]See Book 1, toward the end of Chapter 1: "The ringing cedar".

[11]See Book 2, at the very end of Chapter 31: "How to produce healing cedar oil".

[12]*The soul of Russia sings in Anastasia's ray. A people's book* (Russian title: *V luche Anastasii zvuchit dusha Rossii. Narodnaya kniga*) — a 544-page volume of readers' poetry, art and letters. Seven sample poems from this collection are reproduced in English translation at the end of Book 1, Chapter 30: "Author's message to readers".

allow anyone to edit this. I wrote the preface myself, saying
that the collection was quite an historic publication. I still say
this. How else could one characterise it, containing as it does
letters and musings on life, on the purpose of Man, on what
people today cherish in life. The letters and poems are sincere, and written by people of different ages, different social
situations and religious inclinations. And this book has been
pretty popular. In fact, its popularity has quite given the lie to
the myth that modern Man is interested only in crime novels
and books about sex. People are eager to read poetry — even
if it's not professionally written, but sincere nevertheless.

I've been told on a number of occasions that because I've
thrown out a challenge to the whole brotherhood of the pen
and their erudition, I'm going to be wiped off the face of the
map — nobody will ever recognise me as a writer.

But it wasn't my intention to challenge anyone as a writer.
That was never my intention, but now, when the press is going so far as to attribute the popularity of my books to the
fact that "Russia is a stupid country", and that all my readers
are fools and bigots, I have no choice but to respond to them.
I shall be a writer! I'll do a little more practising, study some
more... I'll ask Anastasia for help... and I shall be a writer! I
shall write new books and reprint the ones already published
in the best printing houses in the world. I shall make the
books about Anastasia and about the people of Russia today
the best books of the millennium.

This is how I shall respond to my present and future critics, but in the meantime I'll simply say this to them:

"To my critics, I bid you farewell. I'm going off with Anastasia — maybe she's a bit naïve, but she's beautiful, kind
and sincere. We shall set off into our new millennium with
more than a million readers in whose hearts a splendid and
inspired image is alive and well. And what is in your hearts,
critics? Phooey on you! Don't come crawling into our new

millennium. Get the... *how can I put it?* Get the hell on back to your own! And even if you do come crawling into ours, you'll only choke on your own anger and envy.

"In our millennium we're seeing the start of a new and splendid co-creation, where the air will be pure and there will be living water and fragrant gardens. And in that millennium I shall continue publishing new collections with readers' poems and letters. I shall call the series *A people's book.* You may say that "the poems therein are horrendous" but I say they are resplendent.

"I shall also put out some audiocassettes with songs of the bards — songs of Soul, of Russia, of Anastasia.[13] You may say that anyone can strum a guitar. But I say that these bards sing from the heart. And I would add, in Anastasia's words: *Not in any of the galaxies could there be found a single string capable of producing a better sound than that of the singing of the human soul.*"[14]

Dear readers, I extend to all of you my heartfelt greetings on the dawn of *our* millennium! On the dawn of your splendid co-creation on the Earth!

Who are we? That is what I have decided to call my next book.

Respectfully,   Vladimir Megré

To be continued...

[13]Over the past five years, over a dozen albums — collections of bards' songs inspired by Anastasia — have been released by the Anastasia Foundation alone, and many more albums have been released independently. A 'Caravan of Love of Sun-bards' (*Karavan Liubvi Solnechnykh bardov*) has also been set up as an itinerant song festival, with large groups of bards travelling from city to city and giving free song performances in Russia and beyond.

[14]See Chapter 6: "Birth".

Hope for the world
Translator's and Editor's Afterword

Wow! Four books translated and counting. Not a bad record, when one considers that just a year ago (as of this writing) not a single page of this series had yet come off the Ringing Cedars presses in America.

The series was launched with the publication of Book 1, *Anastasia*, in February 2005, followed by Book 2, *The Ringing Cedars of Russia*, and Book 3, *The Space of Love*, later in the year. And now *Co-creation* makes four, with at least five volumes still to come. And for this swift progression we have *you* to thank, dear readers, for your ongoing support and encouragement, without which the publication of the new volumes would not have been possible. And needless to say, our gratitude goes out to our original source of support, the One whose inspiration inevitably underlies any legitimate act of 'co-creation'.

Equally noteworthy is the co-creation evident in the evolution of the original series itself, particularly the remarkable transformation of a hard-nosed Siberian commercial trader into one of Russia's bestselling authors. All the more amazing when one remembers that because of Vladimir Megré's initially 'choppy' writing style, the original Russian manuscript of *Anastasia* was rejected by publisher after publisher, leaving him no choice but to bring out the first edition on his own.[1] However, after several print-runs of the self-published *Anastasia* sold out simply by word of mouth, with no advertising campaign or bookstore exposure, professional publishers were

[1]See Book 1, Chapter 30: "Author's message to readers".

only too eager to reconsider, and it was not long before the volumes in the Ringing Cedars Series were selling in the millions. And now in America, as elsewhere in the English-speaking world, *Anastasia* and its sequels are once again running counter to the book-industry's long-held axioms. Even though corporate wholesalers declined to distribute the Ringing Cedars Series to major retailers on the grounds that "no book sells by word of mouth alone, without a budget sufficient for a large advertising campaign", you the readers have proved otherwise, and the books have already spread around the globe without so much as a single advertisement or paid-for review in the press. Many of you have taken it upon yourself to purchase additional copies to give to the family and friends. Some have even gone further and become independent distributors, devoting considerable time and effort to making the books available in your local regions. Thus, as with their original editions, the success of the books in translation is once again the result of the resourcefulness of their readers — readers who have let a new splendid *image* live in their hearts — and the ideas these books set forth are already leaving their mark on the world.

Indeed, there are signs that the world is beginning to grasp the message that there is a better path to freedom, enlightenment and happiness than the one along which it has been hurtling forward at breakneck speed, and that the 'new millennium' on the Earth which Vladimir Megré welcomes on the final pages of *Co-creation* is already dawning with a most glorious radiance. Both in Russia and abroad, Anastasia and the Ringing Cedars Movement are already the subject of many day-to-day conversations and frequent reports in the press (some pertinent examples are detailed below).

Many might find these developments surprising. However, there have been numerous thinkers in both the distant and the recent past who have attempted to send a similar message to humanity: that *it is on the wrong path.* A few of these are worth noting here.

In the late 19th century the great Russian writer Leo Tolstoy took special note of how "millions of people — men, women and children — working ten, twelve or fifteen hours a day, are being transformed into machines and perishing in factories that manufacture unnecessary and harmful gadgets... while more and more villages become deserted". He further observed that "in our time the human heart has been crying out more strongly, more strongly than ever before, against this false life, and calling people to the life demanded by revelation, reason and conscience".[2]

At the same time, on the other side of the Atlantic, religious thinker and Christian Science founder Mary Baker Eddy was calling for a new approach to spiritual freedom from 'mental slavery' to long-held beliefs. She summed up this approach in her major work, *Science and health* (originally published in 1875) as follows: "The despotic tendencies, inherent in mortal mind and always germinating in new forms of tyranny, must be rooted out through the action of the divine Mind".[3]

In 1931 the American prophet Edgar Cayce established his Association for Research and Enlightenment to promote alternative solutions to humanity's problems based on, among other things, personal spirituality and holistic health. Interestingly enough, in one of his many 'readings' he received an intimation that "*on Russia's religious development will come the greater hope of the world*".[4]

---

[2]Leo Tolstoy, *An appeal (Vozzvanie)*, 25 May 1889.

[3]Mary Baker Eddy, *Science and health with key to the Scriptures* (final edition, 1910), p. 225. Not unlike Megré, Eddy frequently used 'divine Mind' (with a capital *M*) as a synonym for God.

[4]From Cayce reading 3976-10 (February 1932). Edgar Cayce Readings are copyrighted (© 1971, 1993–2005) by the Edgar Cayce Foundation. This quotation is used by the kind permission of the copyright holder. Italics ours.

Three years later the world-renowned humanitarian, Dr Albert Schweitzer, re-published the English translation of his book, *On the edge of the primeval forest.* While decrying the injustices inflicted on the indigenous peoples by European settlers,[5] he intimates that the only path to successful colonialism is to turn the indigenous people into more productive workers by *removing them from their native villages, families and plots of land.* Surprisingly, in the same piece Schweitzer even holds labour compulsion (forcing the African native peoples to provide labour in return for material 'benefits' bestowed on them) to be justifiable.[6]

Separating people from their own (or their family's) land is a social trend that goes back centuries. Thomas More described it in Book 1 of his *Utopia* (published in 1516), accusing greedy landowners of taking land from their peasant farmers for their own enrichment. Stalin's forced collectivisation of agriculture in the Soviet Union in the 1930s, the loss of family farms in the United States in the years following World War II and the establishing of huge 'factory farms' in present-day Canada (nearly always achieved by buying up small, family operations at an 'irresistible' price) are further examples of concerted efforts on the part of the 'dark forces' of this world to break Man's ties to the land. This in turn has the effect of subduing his free will and destroying his independence.

---

[5]He writes, for example: "Who can describe the injustice and cruelties that in the course of centuries they [the coloured peoples] have suffered at the hands of Europeans?... If a record could be compiled of all that has happened between the white and the coloured races, it would make a book containing numbers of pages which the reader would have to turn over unread because their contents would be too horrible" — A. Schweitzer, *On the edge of the primeval forest: experiences and observations of a doctor in Equatorial Africa* (London: A.&C. Black Ltd, 1934), p. 115.

[6]See A. Schweitzer, *On the edge of the primeval forest,* pp. 112–118.

All of which gives added weight to Anastasia's proposal, so eloquently set forth by Vladimir Megré in *Co-creation,* of bringing Man (more specifically, a Man's *family*) and his land back together again in the form of what is called in Russian *rodovoe pomestie* — translated in this book as 'family domain' or 'kin's domain'.[7] This phrase is in turn linked, in terms of both meaning and etymology, to the Russian concept of *Rodina,* which has been rendered 'Motherland' in the Ringing Cedars Series, though it is equally translatable as 'native land'.[8]

A brief word on the translation is in order here: inasmuch as both *Rodina* and *rodovoe pomestie* convey concepts that have deep roots in the Russian historical context, unparalleled in Western cultures, a good deal of thought — not to mention countless paragraphs of text and e-mail correspondence — has gone into selecting the most appropriate English equivalents.[9]

We were aided in this decision in part by two of our readers who were asked to voice their thoughts on the selection of an equivalent for *Rodina.* Here is a brief excerpt from each of their responses:

To me *Motherland* seems to invoke the most profound connection one can have to the land. It is the land in which

---

[7]This proposal of Anastasia's — a 'family domain' comprising one hectare of land — is presented throughout the latter part of *Co-creation,* beginning with Chapter 24: "Take back your Motherland, people!". The origin of the Russian term rendered *family domain* (or *kin's domain*) is discussed in footnote 7 in Chapter 33: "School, or the lessons of the gods".

[8]For further discussion of the original meaning of *Rodina,* please see footnote 1 in Chapter 24: "Take back your Motherland, people!".

[9]Even then the final results were, shall we say, less than unanimous, and involved a significant element of compromise on the part of both editor and translator. We can only hope our readers will be able to glean at least a glimmer of understanding from the choices we eventually decided upon.

you were likely born. But even more so, it is the land to which you have bonded through work, toil, sweat and blood, laughter, joy and sustenance.

I like *motherland*. It brings the "life giving" nature of the earth to my heart, "my mother", evoking feelings of tenderness and responsibility. There is much meaning to women in the idea of being a mother and a common thread which relates to my personal life's experience and has a place in the emotional file cabinet of the brain for most people. The relationship between "life" and the earth is shattered in this country [America], as people are so removed from the idea the earth gives us our life.

The linkage made by the latter reader between one's 'personal life' and 'the Earth' is significant. Early in Chapter 24 (appropriately entitled "Take back your Motherland, people!") Anastasia acknowledges that "the whole Earth could be a Motherland [*Rodina*] for each one of its inhabitants", and she designates a family's personal plot of land (subsequently identified as one's *kin's domain*) as a "piece of the Motherland"[10] — thus linking the feelings associated with one's personal family to the broader concept of the family of humanity as a whole. Indeed, perspectives on the concept of the family as revealed in *Co-creation* are by no means confined to the world of the early twenty-first century we call *home,* but reach out in both time and distance to look at *family* not only through the lenses of the past, the present and the future but from beyond our usual sense of planetary space as well.

On this basis, then, it may be seen that the concepts of both *Motherland* and *family domain* reach far beyond the borders of Russia alone. In fact, as indicated above, there are

[10]See Chapter 31: "But who is to blame?".

signs that Anastasia's appeal to "take back your Motherland" is already resonating in the hearts of many people in many parts of the world.

In May 2005, for example, a massive power outage in Moscow reminded many of Anastasia's words concerning the inevitable collapse of artificial life-support systems.[11] This one accident paralysed Russia's capital city for several days in a row and, among other things, resulted in the sewage from millions of dwellings being flushed into the Moskva River untreated. In a radio programme devoted to possible solutions to this problem, one of Russia's most prominent ecologists — and President of the Centre for Russia's Environmental Policy — Academician Alexey Yablokov, made pointed reference not only to E.F. Schumacher's book *Small is Beautiful*[12] but also to the *"hugely popular 'Anastasia' movement of people building their family domains"*.[13]

In neighbouring Latvia, journalist Liudmila Stoma was curious about what was behind a movement of hundreds of people in Latgal Province — "all well-educated specialists in high demand in the labour market" — relocating to a newly formed eco-village in a remote rural area. Upon investigation, she was amazed by what she could only describe as a "new revolution":

> Over the last few years Russia, Belarus and Ukraine have been experiencing a real eco-village boom: thousands of

[11]See, for example, Book 2, Chapter 8: "The answer", and Book 3, Chapter 19: "What to agree with, what to believe?".

[12]E.F. Schumacher, *Small is beautiful: economics as if people mattered* (New York, Harper & Row, 1973).

[13]From Dr Yablokov's interview on ecological threats to Moscow resulting from electricity outages (*Problemy ekologicheskoy bezopasnosti Moskvy v sluchae otkliucheniya podachi elektroenergii*), aired on Radio Svoboda on 25 May 2005. Italics ours.

families are building 'family domains' on one hectare of land each, attaining remarkable self-sufficiency with only sparing use of all the technological achievements of the technocratic world. They are all united by the same goal: to build a Paradise on the Earth. [14]

She ended her article by wondering if "the settlers following Anastasia's advice" in building their own family domains might actually succeed where government subsidies had so miserably failed.

In fact, thousands of new kin's domains are being established each year — not only in Russia and Latvia, but in many other countries as well. And *Dachnik Day* — an annual celebration of our connectedness to Mother Earth on 23 July, the idea of which was proposed in Book 2 (*The Ringing Cedars of Russia*) only eight years ago[15] — has now become an international holiday, and in 2005 it was celebrated for the first time by readers of the series in both America and Canada.

These are but a few examples of a growing, world-wide phenomenon rounded out by international readers' conferences, bards' festivals and multitudes of new poems, songs, paintings and other forms of artistic expression. And already the reaction of readers of the English translation of the series in America, Britain, Canada, Australia, New Zealand and elsewhere is indicating a real 'globalisation' of interest not only in *reading* the Ringing Cedars books, but in *acting on the*

---

[14]Liudmila Stoma, *Vozvrashchenie v Edem* (Return to Eden). *Ezhenedelnik "Vesti"* (Weekly News), n° 8 (601), 24 February 2005. Interestingly enough, Israeli writer and poet Efim Kushner also used the term *revolution* (in the phrase "a global-scale moral revolution") in reference to the Ringing Cedars Series in his book *Beskrovnaya revoliutsiya (A bloodless revolution),* published in 2003.

[15]See Book 2, Chapter 9: "Dachnik Day and an All-Earth holiday!".

ideas they present as well, revealing new manifestations of a Motherland that completely transcends national boundaries.

And to think it all started from a single simple idea, which, multiplied through its first faltering attempts at implementation, still keeps on blossoming and helping people all over the world 'take back' their own Motherland — even as Vladimir Megré's blossoming series of publications started from a single simple proposal to write a book implanted in the thought of an inveterate 'non-writer'. And this former non-writer's initial 'choppy' attempts have now evolved into a flourishing trademark style of poetic prose which characterises Books 3 and 4 of the series. (How well we have succeeded on conveying this evolution of style in the English version, particularly the melodious effect his resulting poetic mode of expression can have on the one who reads it with a heart attuned to textual harmonies, will be up to you the readers to judge.)[16]

As translator and editor we have only to wish you as fascinating an experience in discovering this book on your own as we ourselves had in reading and 'co-translating' it (not to mention 'co-editing' the translation). For now we shall leave you with Anastasia's appeal from Chapter 26 ("Even today everyone can build a home"): "You must feel everything that I outline, and mentally complete yourself the whole design,

---

[16]We are reminded here of the words of British poet Robert Graves: "The reason why the hairs stand on end, the eyes water, the throat is constricted, the skin crawls and a shiver runs down the spine when one writes or reads a true poem is that a true poem is necessarily an invocation of the White Goddess, or Muse, the Mother of All Living...". We feel that this 'goddess' — whom Anastasia calls *Love* — is invoked in this volume with tremendous power. The quote is from Robert Graves, *The White Goddess: a historical grammar of poetic myth* (London: Faber & Faber, 1946; now also published in New York by Noonday Press), pp. 24–25.

and let everyone else draw it along with me. O, God! People, at least give it a try, I beg of you!".

We look forward to meeting you again on the pages of the next book — entitled *Who are we?* — which, like *Co-creation,* will offer ever greater hope for the world.

February 2006

Ottawa, Canada   John Woodsworth

Ozark Mountains, USA   Leonid Sharashkin

THE RINGING CEDARS SERIES AT A GLANCE

Anastasia (ISBN 978-0-9801812-0-3), Book 1 of the Ringing Cedars Series, tells the story of entrepreneur Vladimir Megré's trade trip to the Siberian taiga in 1995, where he witnessed incredible spiritual phenomena connected with sacred 'ringing cedar' trees. He spent three days with a woman named Anastasia who shared with him her unique outlook on subjects as diverse as gardening, child-rearing, healing, Nature, sexuality, religion and more. This wilderness experience transformed Vladimir so deeply that he abandoned his commercial plans and, penniless, went to Moscow to fulfil Anastasia's request and write a book about the spiritual insights she so generously shared with him. True to her promise this life-changing book, once written, has become an international bestseller and has touched hearts of millions of people world-wide.

The Ringing Cedars of Russia (ISBN 978-0-9801812-1-0), Book 2 of the Series, in addition to providing a fascinating behind-the-scenes look at the story of how *Anastasia* came to be published, offers a deeper exploration of the universal concepts so dramatically revealed in Book 1. It takes the reader on an adventure through the vast expanses of space, time and spirit — from the Paradise-like glade in the Siberian taiga to the rough urban depths of Russia's capital city, from the ancient mysteries of our forebears to a vision of humanity's radiant future.

The Space of Love (ISBN 978-0-9801812-2-7), Book 3 of the Series, describes the author's second visit to Anastasia. Rich with new revelations on natural child-rearing and alternative education, on the spiritual significance of breast-feeding and the meaning of ancient megaliths, it shows how each person's thoughts can influence the destiny of the entire Earth and describes practical ways of putting Anastasia's vision of happiness into practice. Megré shares his new outlook on education and children's real creative potential after a visit to a school where pupils build their own campus and cover the ten-year Russian school programme in just two years. Complete with an account of an armed intrusion into Anastasia's habitat, the book highlights the limitless power of Love and non-violence.

Co-creation (ISBN 978-0-9801812-3-4), Book 4 and centrepiece of the Series, paints a dramatic living image of the creation of the Universe and humanity's place in this creation, making this primordial mystery relevant to our everyday living today. Deeply metaphysical yet at the same time down-to-Earth practical, this poetic heart-felt volume helps us uncover answers to the most significant questions about the essence and meaning of the Universe and the nature and purpose of our existence. It also shows how and why the knowledge of these answers, innate in every human being, has become obscured and forgotten, and points the way toward reclaiming this wisdom and — in partnership with Nature — manifesting the energy of Love through our lives.

Who Are We? (ISBN 978-0-9801812-4-1), Book 5 of the Series, describes the author's search for real-life 'proofs' of Anastasia's vision presented in the previous volumes. Finding these proofs and taking stock of ongoing global environmental destruction, Vladimir Megré describes further practical steps for putting Anastasia's vision into practice. Full of beautiful realistic images of a new way of living in co-operation with the Earth and each other, this book also highlights the role of children in making us aware of the precariousness of the present situation and in leading the global transition toward a happy, violence-free society.

The Book of Kin (ISBN 978-0-9801812-5-8), Book 6 of the Series, describes another visit by the author to Anastasia's glade in the Siberian taiga and his conversations with his growing son, which cause him to take a new look at education, science, history, family and Nature. Through parables and revelatory dialogues and stories Anastasia then leads Vladimir Megré and the reader on a shocking re-discovery of the pages of humanity's history that have been distorted or kept secret for thousands of years. This knowledge sheds light on the causes of war, oppression and violence in the modern world and guides us in preserving the wisdom of our ancestors and passing it over to future generations.

The Energy of Life (ISBN 978-0-9801812-6-5), Book 7 of the Series, re-asserts the power of human thought and the influence of our

thinking on our lives and the destiny of the entire planet and the
Universe. It also brings forth a practical understanding of ways to
consciously control and build up the power of our creative thought.
The book sheds still further light on the forgotten pages of humanity's history, on religion, on the roots of inter-racial and inter-
religious conflict, on ideal nutrition, and shows how a new way of
thinking and a lifestyle in true harmony with Nature can lead to
happiness and solve the personal and societal problems of crime,
corruption, misery, conflict, war and violence.

The New Civilisation (ISBN 978-0-9801812-7-2), Book 8, Part 1 of the
Series, describes yet another visit by Vladimir Megré to Anastasia
and their son, and offers new insights into practical co-operation
with Nature, showing in ever greater detail how Anastasia's lifestyle
applies to our lives. Describing how the visions presented in previous volumes have already taken beautiful form in real life and produced massive changes in Russia and beyond, the author discerns
the birth of a new civilisation. The book also paints a vivid image of
America's radiant future, in which the conflict between the powerful and the helpless, the rich and the poor, the city and the country,
can be transcended and thereby lead to transformations in both the
individual and society.

Rites of Love (ISBN 978-0-9801812-8-9), Book 8, Part 2, contrasts
today's mainstream attitudes to sex, family, childbirth and education with our forebears' lifestyle, which reflected their deep spiritual understanding of the significance of conception, pregnancy,
homebirth and upbringing of the young in an atmosphere of love.
In powerful poetic prose Megré describes their ancient way of life,
grounded in love and non-violence, and shows the practicability of
this same approach today. Through the life-story of one family, he
portrays the radiant world of the ancient Russian Vedic civilisation,
the drama of its destruction and its re-birth millennia later — in our
present time.

Vladimir Megré
The Ringing Cedars Series

Translated from the Russian by **John Woodsworth**
Edited by **Dr Leonid Sharashkin**

- Book 1 **Anastasia**
  ISBN: 978-0-9801812-0-3

- Book 2 **The Ringing Cedars of Russia**
  ISBN: 978-0-9801812-1-0

- Book 3 **The Space of Love**
  ISBN: 978-0-9801812-2-7

- Book 4 **Co-creation**
  ISBN: 978-0-9801812-3-4

- Book 5 **Who Are We?**
  ISBN: 978-0-9801812-4-1

- Book 6 **The Book of Kin**
  ISBN: 978-0-9801812-5-8

- Book 7 **The Energy of Life**
  ISBN: 978-0-9801812-6-5

- Book 8, Part 1 **The New Civilisation**
  ISBN: 978-0-9801812-7-2

- Book 8, Part 2 **Rites of Love**
  ISBN: 978-0-9801812-8-9

RINGING
CEDARS
PRESS

Published by **Ringing Cedars Press**
www.ringingcedars.com